EYEWITNESS TRAVEL

TOP 10 BRUSSELS

BRUGES, ANTWERP & GHENT

WITHDRAWN ANTONY MASON

Top 10 Brussels, Bruges, Antwerp & Ghent Highlights

The Top 10 of Everything

CONTENTS

Brussels, Bruges, Antwerp & Ghent Area by Area

Streetsmart

Within each Top 10 list in this book, no hierarchy of quality or popularity is implied. All 10 are, in the editor's opinion, of roughly equal merit.

Front cover and spine Buildings in the Grand Place, Brussels
Back cover A canal scene in Bruges
Title page The Belfort and the Dijver canal, as seen from Rozenhoedkaai, Bruges

Welcome to
Brussels, Bruges, Antwerp & Ghent

Brussels, capital of Europe, and the three great cities of Flanders offer an extraordinarily rich spread of rewards. Fabulous art, trend-setting design and fashion, outstanding restaurants, some of the world's best beer and chocolate, and a heritage that has flourished since the Golden Age. With this Eyewitness Top 10 guide, it's yours to explore.

The splendours of that Golden Age are showcased in the paintings of Jan van Eyck, Hans Memling and their contemporaries in the great art collections of all the cities, such as the **Musées Royaux des Beaux-Arts** in Brussels and the **Groeningemuseum** in Bruges. This artistic brilliance soared again to new heights with Rubens, whose grand home and studio, the **Rubenshuis**, is one of the treasures of Antwerp. Architecture tracks a parallel path, with medieval squares such as the **Burg** in Bruges, the Gothic **Antwerp Cathedral**, and the splendid Gothic and Flemish Baroque **Grand Place** in Brussels.

Cultural attractions apart, these are also walkable cities, adapted for modern living, with elegant shopping streets, lively cafés, star-spangled restaurants – and the world's best twice-fried *frites*.

Whether you're coming for a weekend or a week, our Top 10 guide explores the best of everything these cities can offer, from the glass trumpets of the **Musée des Instruments de Musique** in Brussels and the cutting-edge contemporary art of the **SMAK** gallery in Ghent, to the enchanting backwaters of Eastern Bruges and the throbbing clubs of Antwerp. There are tips throughout, from seeking out what's free to finding the liveliest festivals, plus easy-to-follow itineraries, designed to tie together the must-see sights in a short space of time. Add inspiring photography and detailed maps, and you've got the essential pocket-sized travel companion. **Enjoy the book, and enjoy Brussels, Bruges, Antwerp and Ghent.**

Clockwise from top: Lier near Antwerp; Blinde Ezelstraat, Bruges; Grand Place, Brussels; Le Botanique, Brussels; Rodin's *The Thinker*, Brussels; waffles; Comics Art Museum, Brussels

Exploring Brussels, Bruges, Antwerp & Ghent

With so much on offer, these cities are at their best day and night, and there is much to see beyond the main museums and attractions. Part of the pleasure is ambling about the pedestrian-friendly streets and savouring time spent in the restaurants and cafés. These two- and seven-day itineraries will help you make the most of these four fascinating Belgian cities.

Key
— Two-day itinerary
— Seven-day itinerary

The Grand Place is dominated by Brussels' magnificent town hall.

Two Days in Brussels

Day ❶
MORNING
Start at the **Grand Place** (see pp14–15). Walk through the **Galeries Royales Saint-Hubert** (see p77) to reach the **Cathédrale des Saints Michel et Gudule** (see p74).

AFTERNOON
After lunch, head to the **Musée des Instruments de Musique** (see pp20–21; closed Mon) and the **Musées Royaux des Beaux-Arts** (see pp18–19; closed Mon).

Day ❷
MORNING
Visit **La Bourse** (see p16), and walk via the Place Sainte-Catherine to the

Musées Royaux des Beaux-Arts is made up of three integrated museums.

Église St-Jean-Baptiste au Béguinage *(see p75)*. Wander the **Place des Martyrs** *(see p76)* on the way to the **Comics Art Museum** *(see pp26–7; closed Mon)*

AFTERNOON
Take a tram to the **Horta Museum** *(see pp22–3; closed Mon)*. Wander the Art Nouveau streets around here.

Seven Days in Brussels, Bruges, Ghent and Antwerp

BRUSSELS – Day ❶
As day one of Two Days in Brussels.

BRUGES – Day ❷
MORNING
Go to the **Markt** and climb the **Belfort** *(see p91)* for a panoramic view. After, head for the **Burg** *(see pp28–9)*.
AFTERNOON
Walk to **Groeningemuseum** *(see pp30–31; closed Mon)*, with its outstanding collection of Flemish masters. Explore the **Onze-Lieve-Vrouwekerk** *(see p92)* and then the **Sint-Janshospitaal** *(see p92; closed Mon)*. Walk on to the **Begijnhof** *(see p93)*.

BRUGES – Day ❸
MORNING
Begin at **Choco-Story** and/or the **Frietmuseum** *(see p94)*, then walk via

the **Sint-Walburgakerk** *(see p94)* into the pleasantly quiet district of **Eastern Bruges** *(see p95)* to visit the **Sint-Annakerk** and the **Volkskundemuseum** *(closed Mon)*.
AFTERNOON
Spend the afternoon at the extraordinary **Jeruzalemkapel** *(closed Sun)* and the neighbouring **Kantcentrum** *(see p95)*, the lace centre, which has demonstrations in the afternoon. Finish by exploring the streets of Eastern Bruges further.

Jeruzalemkapel is a 15th-century hidden gem next to the Kantcentrum.

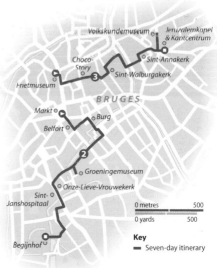

Key
■■ Seven-day itinerary

0 metres   500
0 yards   500

Exploring Brussels, Bruges, Antwerp & Ghent

Korenlei, one of Antwerp's attractive quays, is a pick-up point for boat trips.

Seven Days in Brussels, Bruges, Ghent and Antwerp

GHENT – Day ❹

MORNING

Pay a pilgrimage to *The Adoration of the Mystic Lamb* (see pp32–3), then go to the Sint-Michielsbrug on the **Graslei and Korenlei** (see p109) for the views. Visit the **Design Museum** (see p111; closed Mon).

AFTERNOON

Take a canal trip, visit **Huis van Alijn** folklore museum (see p110; closed Mon), then wander around the quaint **Patershol** district (see p54) behind the museum.

GHENT – Day ❺

MORNING

Take a tram to Ghent's two great art galleries, **MSK** and **SMAK** (see p111; closed Mon).

AFTERNOON

Walk back across the Citadelpark to visit the **STAM** city museum (see p110; closed Mon) before returning to the historic city centre.

Key

■ Seven-day itinerary

0 metres 500
0 yards 500

The Adoration of the Mystic Lamb is the star attraction in the Sint-Baafskathedraal in Ghent.

Antwerp Cathedral dominates the medieval market square.

ANTWERP – Day ❻

MORNING

Admire the guildhouses and town hall in the **Grote Markt** *(see p101)*, then walk to **Antwerp Cathedral** *(see pp34–5)*. Visit the Museum Vleeshuis *(see p102; closed Mon–Wed)*.

AFTERNOON

Visit the **Sint-Pauluskerk** *(see p104)*, then continue further north to the dockside **Museum Aan de Stroom** *(see p102; closed Mon)*.

ANTWERP – Day ❼

MORNING

To avoid the crowds, get an early start at the **Rubenshuis** *(see pp36–7; closed Mon)*. Continue to the **Museum Mayer van den Bergh** *(see p102; closed Mon)*.

AFTERNOON

Take in some radical contemporary art at **MUKHA** gallery *(see p104; closed Mon)*, and visit the nearby **FotoMuseum Provincie Antwerpen (FoMu)** *(see p104; closed Mon)*. To finish your trip, head back to the old city centre via the **Museum Plantin-Moretus** *(see p102; closed Mon)*

FotoMuseum Provincie (FoMu) covers every aspect of photography.

Key

■ Seven-day itinerary

Top 10 Brussels, Bruges, Antwerp & Ghent Highlights

The magnificent architecture on display in the Grand Place, Brussels

TOP 10 Brussels, Bruges, Antwerp & Ghent Highlights

The four great cities of northern Belgium share a rich cultural heritage, yet they are very different. Each, in its own way, is hugely rewarding – not only in cultural sights, but also in delightful and welcoming places to stay, eat and drink.

1 The Grand Place, Brussels

For architectural theatre, the centrepiece of Brussels is hard to beat – as it was three centuries ago (see pp14–15).

2 Musées Royaux des Beaux-Arts, Brussels

Rubens, Van Dyke, Magritte – this splendid collection reveals some of art's greatest names (see pp18–19).

3 Musée des Instruments de Musique, Brussels

Housed in a magnificent Art Nouveau building, the "mim" contains thousands of instruments (see pp20–21).

4 Horta Museum, Brussels

Victor Horta was the original Art Nouveau architect; his own house is an expression of this and preserved as a shrine to Art Nouveau (see pp22–3).

5 Comics Art Museum, Brussels

Dedicated to the comic strip, this place reveals all there is to know about this very Belgian art form: Tintin and beyond (see pp26–7).

The Burg, Bruges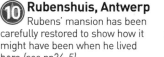

The old centre of Bruges is an architectural gem – a small, intimate square surrounded by historic gabled buildings, each one embellished with fascinating detail *(see pp28–9).*

7 Groeningemuseum and Sint-Janshospitaal, Bruges

Great Flemish artists of the early 15th century were among the first to perfect oil painting. These two collections demonstrate their extraordinary skills, *(see pp30–31).*

The Adoration of the Mystic Lamb, Ghent 8

This multi-panel altarpiece created in 1426–32 by Jan van Eyck and his brother Hubrecht is a great cultural treasure of Europe *(see pp36–7).*

10 Rubenshuis, Antwerp

Rubens' mansion has been carefully restored to show how it might have been when he lived here *(see pp34–5).*

Antwerp Cathedral 9

Antwerp's cathedral is the city's main landmark, and the largest Gothic church in Belgium. Its impressive interior has some exceptional triptychs *(see pp32–3).*

🔟⭐ The Grand Place, Brussels

Brussels' Grand Place is the focal point of the city, a tirelessly uplifting masterpiece of unified architecture. Full of symbolic sculpture and gilding, for centuries this was the economic and administrative heart of the city. It was the setting for markets, fairs, pageants and jousts, for the proclamation of decrees, and for public executions. Even without its old political and economic prestige and the bustle of through-traffic, it still hums with activity.

5 Hôtel de Ville

The Town Hall was the first major building on the Grand Place. Largely rebuilt since its 15th-century beginnings, it still has its original spire, with a statue of St Michael killing the devil.

1 Le Cornet

This elaborate building (No 6) was once the guildhouse of the boatmen. Its adornments include a top storey resembling the stern of a ship **(above)**.

2 Le Cygne

"The Swan" (No 9) was rebuilt as a private residence in 1698, but in 1720 it was acquired by the Guild of Butchers. It later became a café, and Karl Marx held meetings of the German Workers' Party here.

3 Le Renard

No 7 was a guildhouse *(gildehuis)* – the prestigious headquarters of the Guild of Haberdashers. A gilded statue of a fox **(right)** sits above the door, reflecting the building's old name (Le Renard).

4 Maison des Brasseurs

Called l'Arbre d'Or (the Golden Tree), the brewers' guildhouse (No 10) was designed by Guillaume de Bruyn. It is still used by the Confédération des Brasseurs, and houses a small museum of brewing **(left)**.

NEED TO KNOW
MAP C3

Hôtel de Ville: guided tours start 2pm Wed, 11am, 3pm & 4pm Sun; arrive 15 minutes before. 02 548 04 47. Tour: €5.

Maison du Roi (Musée de la Ville de Bruxelles): 10am–5pm Tue–Sun. 02 279 43 50. Adm: €8.

Maison des Brasseurs (Musée de la Brasserie): 10am–5pm daily. 02 511 49 87. Adm: €5

■ There are two famous bar-restaurants here – both pricey, but worth it for their Bruxellois style: Le Roy d'Espagne at No 1, and La Chaloupe d'Or at Nos 24–25. Le Cygne has a famous restaurant upstairs and the Brasserie l'Ommegang downstairs.

■ A tourist office in the Hôtel de Ville is useful for information.

6 Maison du Roi

This medieval-style "King's House", built in the 1870s, houses the Musée de la Ville de Bruxelles, a miscellany of city history, including costumes designed for the Manneken-Pis statue.

8 The Tapis de Fleurs

Every even-numbered year for five days in mid-August, the Grand Place is taken over by a massive floral display known as the Carpet of Flowers (below).

NOT QUITE THE REAL THING

The guildhouses of the Grand Place are built largely in the Flemish Renaissance style of the late 16th and early 17th centuries. Little of it actually dates from this period, however. On 13–14 August 1695, under the orders of Louis XIV, French troops led by Marshal de Villeroy lined up their cannons, took aim at the spire of the Hôtel de Ville, and pulverized the city centre. In defiance, the citizens set about reconstructing the Grand Place, a task that was completed in just five years.

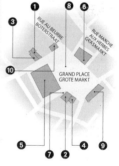

7 Statue of Everard 't Serclaes

Everard 't Serclaes died on this site in 1388 resisting Flemish occupation. Superstitious passers-by stroke the limbs of his bronze statue (below) for luck.

9 Maison des Ducs de Brabant

The south-eastern flank of this impressive Neo-Classical building was originally conceived (in 1698) as a single block of seven units by Guillaume de Bruyn.

10 Maison des Boulangers

The bakers' guildhouse is coated with symbols, including six figures representing the essential elements of breadmaking. The unusual octagonal lantern on the roof is topped by a striking gilded statue of Fame.

Around the Grand Place

Restaurants line Rue des Bouchers

1 Rue des Bouchers
MAP C3

Many of the streets around the Grand Place reflect the trades that once operated there. The "Street of the Butchers" and its intersecting Petite Rue des Bouchers are famous for their lively restaurants and colourful displays of food.

2 Musée du Costume et de la Dentelle
MAP C3 ▪ Rue de la Violette 12 ▪ 02 213 44 50 ▪ Open 10am–5pm Tue–Sun ▪ Adm

This small but rewarding museum dedicated to historic costume and lace has a limited but choice selection of exhibits.

3 La Bourse
MAP B3 ▪ Bruxella 1238 ▪ 02 279 43 55 ▪ Guided tours first Wed of month (10:15am for tours in English; departs from outside Maison du Roi on the Grand Place)

The Stock Exchange is an unmistakable feature of the Brussels landscape. Built in 1873 in the style of a Greek temple and lavishly decorated, it is now used by Euronext (European stock

Detail on the façade of La Bourse

markets) and functions as an occasional exhibition space. Beneath it are the exposed archaeological remains of a convent founded in 1238, known as Bruxella 1238.

4 Manneken-Pis
MAP B3 ▪ corner of Rue de l'Étuve and Rue du Chêne

No one knows why this bronze statue of a boy peeing water has become such a symbol of Brussels. Since the early 18th century, costumes of all kinds have been made for him.

Galeries Royales Saint-Hubert

5 Galeries Royales Saint-Hubert
MAP C3

Built in 1847, this was the first shopping arcade in Europe. It boasts magnificent vaulted glass ceilings.

6 Place Saint-Géry
MAP B3

The square that marks the site of Brussels' first settlement is today dominated by Les Halles de Saint-Géry, an attractive iron and red-brick structure built in 1881 as a meat market. Now a craft market, exhibition space and café, it is the central focus of an area known for its nightlife.

7 Maison Dandoy
MAP C3 ▪ Rue au Beurre 31

Brussels´ best makers of biscuits have been perfecting their craft since 1829. Behind a ravishing shop window lie goodies such as *speculoos*, *sablés* and waffles.

8 Statue of Charles Buls
MAP C3

In Place Agora is one of Brussels´ most delightful statues: a portrait of the bearded and moustachioed artist, scholar and reformer Charles Buls (1837–1914) and his dog. Buls, who served as Burgomaster from 1891 to 1899, is credited with restoring the Grand Place.

9 Église Notre-Dame de Bon Secours
MAP B3 ▪ Rue du Marché au Charbon 91 ▪ 02 514 31 13 ▪ Open daily Jun–Nov: 9:30am–6pm, Dec–May: 10am–5pm

The most striking feature of this delightful church, built in 1664–94, is its soaring hexagonal choir, rising to

Église Notre-Dame de Bon Secours

a domed ceiling. The façade bears the coat of arms of the enlightened 18th-century governor of the Austrian Netherlands, Charles of Lorraine.

10 Église Saint-Nicolas
MAP C3 ▪ Rue au Beurre 1 ▪ 02 513 80 22 ▪ Open 8am–6:30pm Mon–Fri, 9am–6pm Sat, 9am–7:30pm Sun

St Nicholas of Myra – aka Santa Claus – was patron saint of merchants, and this church has served the traders of the Grand Place since the 14th century. It retains a fine medieval atmosphere, despite desecration by Protestant rebels in the 16th century and damage during the bombardment of 1695.

THE ÎLE SAINT-GÉRY AND THE RIVER SENNE

Brussels began as a group of little islands on a marshy river. Legend has it that in the 6th century AD, St Géry, Bishop of Cambrai, founded a church here, and a settlement grew around it. The name Broeksele (later Brussels), meaning "house in the swamp", is first mentioned in 966, and a castle was built on the island by Charles, Duke of Lorraine, a decade later, effectively launching the city. The river, called the Senne, ran through the city until the 19th century. Never large, it became overwhelmed by the growing population, and such a health hazard that it was covered over in 1867–71. This process created Boulevard Anspach and Boulevard Adolphe Max, among others, while the river formed part of the city´s new sewer and drainage system. It can still be glimpsed here and there in the city.

The River Senne in 1587

TOP 10 ⭐ Musées Royaux des Beaux-Arts

Brussels' "Royal Museums of the Fine Arts" are a *tour de force*. Many of the great names in art history are represented here. The galleries are divided into three integrated parts: the Old Masters Museum (15th to 18th centuries), the Fin-de-Siècle Museum (19th and early 20th centuries) and the Magritte Museum. Overall, they represent one of the greatest and most comprehensive collections of art from the Low Countries anywhere in the world.

Realism to Post-Impressionism (Fin-de-Siècle Museum)

1 Belgian artists echoed French art movements, but applied their own originality. Social Realism emanates from works by Hippolyte Boulenger; Émile Claus's bucolic scenes reflect the late-Impressionist style, Luminism; Henri Evenepoel's Post-Impressionist style is redolent of Degas; James Ensor prefigured the Expressionists **(right)**.

3 Gillian Crowet Collection (Fin-de-Siècle Museum)

This outstanding collection showcases the work of Art Nouveau masters such as Victor Horta, Émile Gallé, Alphonse Mucha and Fernand Khnopff **(below)**.

2 Early Netherlandish Painting (Old Masters Museum)

One of the most precious parts of the collection: extraordinary work by Rogier van der Weyden **(above)**, Hans Memling, Dirk Bouts and Petrus Christus. The "Flemish Primitives" perfected the technique of oil painting, and had a major influence on Italian art.

4 Old Masters Museum

This extraordinarily rich collection spans the 15th to the 18th centuries, and includes the Flemish Primitives and the Golden Age of Rubens, Van Dyck and Jordaens. Although primarily focusing on Belgian art, it also has work by major European painters such as Claude Lorrain, Tiepolo and Jacques-Louis David (including his *Death of Marat*).

⑤ Magritte Museum

René Magritte's work **(above)** is so often seen in reproduction that it is a treat to see it up close. The museum, in a separate part of the Musées Royaux des Beaux-Arts, houses the world's largest collection of his work.

⑥ Fin-de-Siècle Museum

This museum embraces not just painting and sculpture, but early Art Nouveau artifacts and architecture from 1884 to 1914.

⑦ The Modern Collection

The museum has a fine collection of 20th- and 21st-century art **(below)** but this is due to move to the Vanderborght building, in 2018. Until then, some items are on show in the Patio.

⑧ The Rubens Collection (Old Masters Museum)

To those who think of Rubens only in terms of scenes filled with plump, naked ladies, this collection comes as a revelation, displaying vigour, spontaneity and artistic risk-taking.

⑨ The Buildings

Set on the crest of the Coudenberg, the old royal enclave of Brussels, the museum's main buildings were designed by one of the leading architects of the day, Belgian Alphonse Balat (1818–95).

⑩ Belgian Symbolism (Fin-de-Siècle Museum)

Look out for the inventiveness and skill of such artists as Léon Spilliaert, Jean Delville and Léon Frédéric.

■ The museums have their own cafeteria, but far more exciting is the mim restaurant on top of the nearby Musée des Instruments de Musique *(see pp20–21)*. Also, just a short walk away, are the cafés of the Place du Grand Sablon, including the exquisite *chocolatier* Wittamer *(see p78)*.

■ The museums tend to be quieter mid-week during the middle of the day, so this can be the ideal time for a more leisurely visit.

Gallery Guide
The Old Masters Museum is set out in sequence on a single, extensive upper floor of the building. The Fin-de-Siècle Museum occupies a spiralling sunken building originally built to house the modern art collection. The Magritte Museum is on five floors in an adjacent building. Visitors can choose to visit each of these individually, but it is far cheaper to buy a "combi" ticket, which permits entry to all.

TOP 10 ★ Musée des Instruments de Musique

The Musée des Instruments de Musique, often referred to as "Le mim", exhibits musical instruments from ancient to modern, including the largest collection of instruments by Adolphe Sax. The exhibits – selected from a collection totalling more than 7,000 pieces – are beautifully arranged, and headphones permit visitors to hear what the instruments actually sound like. The museum is housed in an exhilarating location: the classic Art Nouveau department store called "Old England".

1 The "Old England" Building

Completed in 1899, this is a classic example of the innovative iron-and-glass structures produced by Art Nouveau architects **(below)**. The interior is equally impressive.

3 Stringed Instruments

Sharing the 2nd floor is the stringed instrument section, including violins **(right)**, psalteries, dulcimers, harps, lutes and guitars, plus a recon-struction of a violin workshop.

4 20th-Century Instruments

Technology has had a major impact on music in the late 20th century, from electric amplification to synthesizers and computer-generated music. This small collection offers a fascinating snapshot. If you don't know what an *ondes martenot* is, here's your chance to find out.

6 Mechanical Instruments

The ingenuity of instrument-makers is most evident in this collection, which includes some outrageously elaborate musical boxes and a *carillon* – a set of bells used to play tunes.

5 Non-European Instruments

The mim runs a strong line in ethnomusicology. This impressive collection includes panpipes, sitars, African harps and drums, gamelan orchestras, and giant Tibetan horns **(below)**.

2 The Historical Survey

This section charts the evolution of western "art" instruments from antiquity through the Renaissance to the 19th century. The headphone guide shows the evolving complexity of musical sound.

7 mim Restaurant

Even if you don't need refuelling, take the lift up to the 10th floor to admire the view. From here you can see the statue of St Michael on the top of the spire of the Hôtel de Ville in the Grand Place, and far across town to the Basilique Nationale and the Atomium.

Trombone with six valves

10 Visitor Guidance System

A guidance system is given to visitors; as you approach some instruments, recordings and images of those exhibits are triggered.

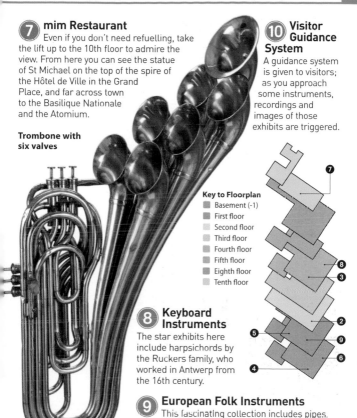

Key to Floorplan

- ■ Basement (-1)
- ■ First floor
- ■ Second floor
- ■ Third floor
- ■ Fourth floor
- ■ Fifth floor
- ■ Eighth floor
- ■ Tenth floor

8 Keyboard Instruments

The star exhibits here include harpsichords by the Ruckers family, who worked in Antwerp from the 16th century.

9 European Folk Instruments

This fascinating collection includes pipes, rattles, accordions, hurdy-gurdies and some splendid oddities – chief among them a collection of Belgian glass trumpets.

NEED TO KNOW

MAP D4 ■ Rue Montagne de la Cour 2 ■ 02 545 01 30 ■ www.mim.be

Open 9:30am–5pm Tue–Fri, 10am–5pm Sat–Sun

Adm: €8 (free on first Wed of every month after 1pm)

■ mim Restaurant, on the top floor of the museum, serves reasonably priced light lunch dishes such as sandwiches, pasta and a selection of salads. If this is too busy, you can head off to the cafés of the Place du Grand Sablon, just a short walk away.

■ Expect to spend at least two hours in this museum; to do it full justice, give it three to four hours. Although the Museum closes at 5pm, staff like to empty the exhibition rooms by 4:45pm.

Museum Guide

The museum is set out on four of the building's ten floors. Floor −1 is called "Musicus mechanicus" and features mechanical, electrical and electronic instruments. The 1st floor covers instruments of the world. The 2nd floor is a historical survey of western instruments, from Egyptian origins to 19th-century innovations. The 4th floor is used to show parts of the permanent collection and for temporary exhibitions. There is a shop on the 3rd floor, library on the 5th, and a concert hall on the 8th; the restaurant is on the top floor.

🔟 ⭐ Horta Museum, Brussels

In the late 19th century, Brussels was a centre for avant-garde design, and a rapidly growing city. To feed the market for stylish mansions, architects scavenged history for ideas; the result was the so-called "eclectic style". In 1893, architect Victor Horta created a new style – later labelled "Art Nouveau" – full of free-flowing, naturalistic lines, elaborated with wrought iron, stained glass, mosaics, murals and finely crafted woodwork. Horta brought this style to full maturity when he built his house – now this museum.

The Building ①
When designing for his clients, Horta liked to tailor the house to how they lived. His own house **(right)** has two distinct parts: on the left his residence; on the right, his offices and studio.

② Furniture
Horta also liked to design the furniture to go in his houses. Although it bears an Art Nouveau stamp, Horta's furniture tends to be simple, restrained and practical.

③ Woodwork
There is a note of austerity as well as luxury in Art Nouveau design. The richly carved wood in the dining room is left natural, allowing the quality of the wood to speak for itself.

⑥ Scale Model of the Maison du Peuple
Horta was well-known for his designs for commercial and public buildings. The Maison du Peuple was an innovative cast-iron structure built for the Société Coopérative in 1895. A scale model of it can be seen in the cellar.

④ Art Nouveau Sculpture Collection
Throughout the museum are fine sculptures by late 19th-century Belgian artists. Look out for *La Ronde des Heures* **(below)**, in the rear salon on the first floor. This intriguing little bronze was created by Philippe Wolfers (1858–1929), a leading Art Nouveau jeweller and silversmith who worked with Horta.

⑤ Structural Ironwork
In what was considered a bold gesture at the time, Horta used iron structures to support his houses. He even made a virtue of it, by leaving some of the iron exposed and drawing attention to it with wrought-iron embellishments **(left)**.

⑦ Leaded Glass
The use of stained glass – shapes of coloured glass held together by lead strips – was embraced by Art Nouveau architects. Examples appear at various points in the house – notably in the door panels and stairwell skylight.

8 Mosaics

The sinuous lines of Art Nouveau design in the mosaic tiling of the dining room floor **(left)** help to soften the effect of the white-enamelled industrial brick lining that covers the walls.

9 The Staircase

The interior design hangs on a central stairwell, lit from the top by a large, curving skylight. The ironwork bannisters have been given a typically exuberant flourish **(above)**.

Fixtures and Fittings 10

Horta was an *ensemblier*: he liked to design an entire building in all its detail, down to the last light fixture **(right)**, door handle and coat hook. This attention to detail conveys the impression of complete architectural mastery: nothing is left to chance.

VICTOR HORTA

The son of a Ghent shoemaker, Victor Horta (1861–1947) studied architecture from the age of 13. After designing the Hôtel Tassel *(see p48)* in 1893–5, his reputation soared. Thereafter he designed houses, department stores and public buildings. With World War I, Art Nouveau fell from favour, and Horta turned to a harder style, seen in his Palais des Beaux-Arts in Brussels. He was awarded the title of Baron in 1932.

NEED TO KNOW

MAP C8 ■ Rue Américaine 25, 1060 BRU (Saint-Gilles) ■ 02 543 04 90 ■ www.hortamuseum.be

Open 2–5:30pm Tue–Sun. Closed Mon, public hols

Adm: €10

■ There are several bars and cafés nearby, around Place du Châtelain. For a spot of good-value lunch before the museum's 2pm opening hour, try the charming La Canne en Ville *(see p87)*; for somewhere with real design flair, head for Rue du Page and La Quincaillerie, dating from 1903 *(see p87)*.

■ The Horta Museum is at the heart of a cluster of Art Nouveau buildings. Key streets include Rue Defacqz, Rue Faider and Rue Paul-Émile Janson. Hôtel Hannon is also close by *(see pp48–9)*.

Following pages Cathédrale des Saints Michel et Gudule, Brussels

TOP 10 ⭐ Comics Art Museum

Tintin is perhaps the most famous Belgian in the world. But this comic-strip hero is just one of hundreds produced in Belgium over the last century. The comic strip – *bande dessinée* in French – is called the "ninth art". The library at Brussels' Comics Art Museum contains 40,000 volumes. Set out in a renovated fabric warehouse, the museum (formerly called the Centre Belge de la Bande Dessinée) presents the history of the form, shows how strips are made, and explores some of the key characters and their creators.

1 Invention of the Comic Strip

This exhibition explores how the comic strip began **(below)**. Discover the history of the art form and its use by civilizations throughout the world – from early cave art to 19th-century magazines.

4 The Building

The museum **(right)** occupies what was formerly the Magasins Waucquez, an innovative Art Nouveau structure of cast iron supporting large expanses of glass, designed by Victor Horta in 1903–6 (see p49).

2 The Art of the Comic Strip

This exhibition contains a selection of original drawings showing how comic strips are made. A wide range of artists, from the traditional to the modern, donated their sketches and studies to demonstrate each step involved in the process of creating a comic strip.

5 Slumberland Bookshop

Named after the Little Nemo adventure, the shop stocks everything on the comic strip theme.

6 Temporary Exhibitions

A constantly changing space used for exhibitions dedicated to a particular artist, theme or movement within comic strips.

3 Pieter De Poortere Auditorium

Created by Pieter De Poortere, Dickie is a magazine character adopted by the screen. Here you can view comic strip gags and successful cartoons.

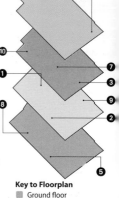

Key to Floorplan
- ▢ Ground floor
- ▢ First floor
- ▢ Second floor
- ▢ Third floor

7 Horta and the Waucquez Warehouse

The exhibition covers the fascinating history of this Art Nouveau former warehouse **(left)**.

8 Library

The library has a public reading room, which is open to anyone with a museum ticket.

TINTIN

The story of Tintin goes back to 1929, when he first appeared in a children's newspaper supplement *Le Petit Vingtième*. Brussels-born inventor Hergé (Georges Rémi, *see p42*) created the character as he took him through a series of adventures related to real events, such as the rise of fascism (*King Ottakar's Sceptre*). The charm of Tintin is his naïve determination, as well as the multitude of archetypal characters that surround him, such as Captain Haddock and his faithful dog Snowy.

9 The Gallery

The Gallery displays a broad range of international albums – both classical and contemporary style. The space is dedicated to new comics from a wide variety of genres from fantasy and satire, to crime and autobiography.

MAP D2 ■ Rue des Sables 20 ■ 02 219 19 80 ■ www.comicscenter.net

NEED TO KNOW

MAP D2 ■ Rue des Sables 20 ■ 02 219 19 80 ■ www.comicscenter.net

Open 10am–6pm Tue–Sun

Adm: €10

∙∙∙∙∙∙∙∙∙∙∙∙∙∙∙∙∙∙∙∙∙∙∙∙∙∙∙∙∙∙∙∙∙

■ The museum's own Brasserie Horta is a convenient place for refreshments and serves a good range of lunch dishes. If that doesn't appeal, you are only a short walk from the Grand Place and its multitude of cafés and restaurants. Nearer at hand is the famous bar À la Mort Subite (*see p78*), a traditional place to sample *gueuze* beer.

■ This museum is *not* guaranteed to entertain children, especially if they do not speak French or Dutch. It is, rather, a museum showing the evolution of the craft. Free guides in English.

10 Tintin

Of course, the main hero of the museum is the famous boy-reporter Tintin, creation of Hergé. Translated into some 40 languages, over 140 million copies of the books have been sold worldwide. The museum acknowledges his status with 3-D models of key characters **(below)**, and the rocket that went to the moon.

🔟⭐ The Burg, Bruges

Bruges began life in the 10th century as a castle built on marshland formed by the River Reie. The castle has disappeared, but the charming square that replaced it, the Burg, has remained the historic heart of the city. The most impressive building is the Stadhuis, a classic late-medieval town hall built when Bruges was a hub of international trade. Just about every century is represented by the buildings on the Burg, which disclose fascinating secrets that lie behind this extraordinary city.

① Breidelstraat

The quaint little street that connects Bruges' main market place, the Markt, to the Burg is lined with shops selling souvenirs as well as one of the city's most famous products, lace.

② Blinde Ezelstraat

A lovely street leads off the south of the Burg, beneath the arch **(above)** that links the Oude Griffie to the Stadhuis. The name "Blind Donkey Street" may relate to a nearby inn.

④ Heilig Bloedbasiliek

On the west side of the Burg is the Basilica of the Holy Blood **(right)**, a chapel lavishly restored in Neo-Gothic style in the late 19th century. Its museum holds a phial of blood said to be Christ's.

③ Renaissancezaal van het Brugse Vrije

In the corner of the Burg is the Renaissance Room, whose star exhibit is the Charles V chimneypiece, a virtuoso piece of 16th-century wood carving.

5 Stadhuis

One of medieval Europe's great secular buildings **(above)**, the Stadhuis (town hall) is an expression of Bruges' self-confidence in medieval times. It was built in 1376–1420 in the aptly named Flamboyant Gothic style.

A bird's-eye view of the Stadhuis and the Burg

6 Proosdij

The Provost's House lining the north side of the Burg is in Flemish Baroque style (1622), with a roof-line balustrade topped by the figure of Justice.

7 Landhuis van het Brugse Vrije

This 18th-century mansion was the head-quarters of the "Liberty of Bruges", an administrative jurisdiction covering a large region around the city, while Bruges governed itself separately.

8 St Basil's Chapel

Beneath the Heilig Bloedbasiliek is another chapel of an utterly contrasting mood. Constructed of hefty grey stone in the 12th century, it is a superb and atmospheric example of muscular Romanesque style, and also a reminder of the Burg's origins as a castle.

9 Oude Civiele Griffie

The Renaissance touched Bruges' architecture only lightly; this "Old Recorders' House", built in 1534–7, is the exception to the rule.

10 The North Side

The little park occupies the site of the Sint-Donaaskerk (see panel). The bronze statue of The Lovers (1986) is by local sculptor Stefaan Depuydt and his wife.

🔟⭐ Two Museums of Bruges

These museums, on separate sites a short distance apart, contain some of the world's finest examples of late medieval art, presenting a selection of work by artists such as Jan van Eyck (c.1390–1441). The Groeningemuseum is a small and charming gallery with a radical edge. The Sint-Janshospitaal, part of the medieval hospital, is devoted to that historic tradition, with the paintings of Hans Memling that were commissioned for its chapel.

1 The Legend of St Ursula

This series of panels by the "Master of the Saint Ursula Legend" tells the popular medieval tale of St Ursula and her company of 11,000 virgins, cruelly martyred in pagan Germany **(left)**.

4 The Last Judgment

Hieronymus Bosch (c.1450–1516) is famous for his nightmarish paintings of spiritual anguish, torture and hell. This example is an insight into the religious psyche of the times.

2 The St Ursula Shrine

Completed by Memling for the Sint-Janshospitaal in 1489, this impressive reliquary **(below)** depicts the Legend of St Ursula in six panels.

3 The Adoration of the Magi

This work, displayed in the Sint-Janshospitaal's chapel, was painted by Memling in 1479. It is known as the Triptych of Jan Floreins after the patron, seen behind a low wall on the left of the central panel **(right)**.

5 The Moreel Triptych

Burgomaster of Bruges, Willem Moreel, commissioned this work from Memling in 1484. Moreel is depicted in the left-hand panel and his wife in the right, with various saints in the middle.

8 Secret-Reflet

This Symbolist work of 1902 by Belgian painter Fernand Khnopff (1858–1921) includes an image of the Sint-Janshospitaal. The title refers to the play on the word "reflection" in the two images.

THE GOLDEN AGE OF BRUGES

Under the dukes of Burgundy Bruges prospered, and in 1429 it became the capital of the Burgundian empire. Its elite became wealthy, educated patrons of the arts. The dukes of Burgundy married into European royalty: Philip the Good married Isabella of Portugal; Charles the Bold, Margaret of York. Their marriages were celebrated with vast feasts – the stuff of European legends. This is the world glimpsed in the paintings of the Flemish masters.

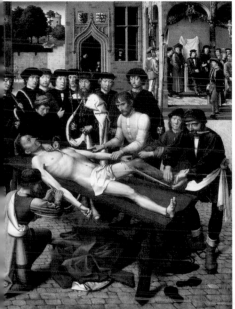

10 Madonna with Canon Joris van der Paele

The supreme masterpiece of the Groeningemuseum collection was painted in 1436 by Jan van Eyck. The detail is astonishing.

6 The Judgment of Cambyses

In 1488, Bruges ill-advisedly imprisoned their ruler, Maximilian, the Holy Roman Emperor. This large diptych by Gerard David depicting the gruesome flaying of a corrupt judge (above) was commissioned for the town hall as a public apology.

9 Martyrdom of Saint Hippolytus

This triptych (c.1468) by Dirk Bouts and Hugo van de Goes, in one scene depicts the saint being pulled apart by four horses – at once horribly gruesome, strangely calm and exquisitely detailed (right).

7 The Triptych with Sts John the Baptist and John the Evangelist

Painted by Memling in 1479, this work celebrates the two St Johns, patron saints of the Sint-Janshospitaal.

🔟⭐ Antwerp Cathedral

Antwerp Cathedral (Onze-Lieve-Vrouwekathedraal) is the largest Gothic church in the Low Countries. Its wedding-cake spire, rising up from a medieval market square, is still a major landmark in the city. The cathedral took 170 years to build, and even then was not complete. It was the church of the wealthy guilds, richly adorned with their shrines, reliquaries and altarpieces. Gutted by fire and vandals in the 16th and 18th centuries, the cathedral still has major treasures, notably two triptychs by Rubens.

1 The Raising of the Cross

This triptych, and the impressive *Descent from the Cross* on the other side of the nave, secured Rubens' reputation in Antwerp. The central and right-hand panels display the dynamic energy that was Rubens' hallmark **(below)**.

2 Original Murals

The cathedral was once bright with murals that have fallen away or been overpainted. Restoration has revealed some of these originals.

3 The Pulpit

Elaborately carved oak pulpits feature in many Belgian churches. The subject of this one, the propagation of the faith in the "four" continents, is tackled with extraordinary ambition – a riot of birds, trees, textile swags, angels, saints and symbolic figures.

4 The Nave

The interior **(above)** is bright and uplifting, largely by virtue of its scale, the expanse of glass, and the soaring space that rises to the rib vaults. Unusually, the columns of the aisle have no capitals, so bend seamlessly to form Gothic arches, creating a serene effect.

5 The Burgundian Window

A fair number of the cathedral's original stained-glass windows have survived. The Burgundian is the oldest window, dating from 1503 **(left)**. It depicts Philip the Handsome, the Duke of Burgundy, and his wife Joanna of Castile, with their patron saints behind them.

The Spire 6

The cathedral's dainty spire **(right)** was built over about 100 years from the mid-1400s onward. As it rises to its pinnacle at 123 m (404 feet), it shows increasingly daring Gothic style. The only other comparable spire is that of the Hôtel de Ville in Brussels.

The Cupola 9

From outside, the dome looks like a tiered black onion. Inside, its logic is clear: the glass tiers let in light to illuminate the *Assumption of the Virgin* (1647), Cornelis Schut's notable ceiling painting. The effect is of looking straight up into the heavens.

The Virgin Exalted through Art 10

In the late 19th century, the cathedral was rescued by restoration. The effort to recreate a medieval effect in some of the chapels behind the choir is admirable. Albrecht De Vriendt's fine triptych shows the "Eyckian" revival at its best.

The Madonna of Antwerp 7

This exceptional wooden statue **(above)** has been a focus of devotion since the 16th century, and has a changing wardrobe of robes and crowns.

The Schyven Organ 8

This impressive instrument is housed in a superb 17th-century case created by three leading sculptors of the day.

Cathedral Floorplan

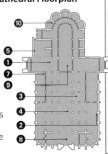

ICONOCLASTS AND FRENCH REVOLUTIONARIES

Antwerp Cathedral was once richly decorated; two episodes have rendered it rather more austere. The first, during the 1560s, was the onslaught of Protestant zealots, or "iconoclasts", who set about ridding churches of statues, paintings and relics. The second occurred in the 1790s, when the forces of the French Revolution went about demolishing churches, or putting them to secular use as stables, barracks, law courts and factories.

NEED TO KNOW

MAP T2
- Handschoenmarkt
- 03 213 99 51
- www.dekathedraal.be

Open 10am–5pm Mon–Fri, 10am–3pm Sat, 1–4pm Sun and public hols

Adm: €6, students and over 60s €4, children under 12 free

- There are many cafés, bars and restaurants in the streets around the cathedral. One tavern, Het Vermoeide Model in Lijnwaadmarkt (see p106), is built against the cathedral walls. Het Kathedraalcafé (see p107) in Torfbrug has a terrace and an inside decorated with statues of saints and religious artifacts.

- Listen out for the 49 carillon bells that play tunes on the hour. In the summer, carillon concerts are given, when the bells are played from a keyboard.

TOP 10 ⭐ Rubenshuis, Antwerp

In 1610, Peter Paul Rubens (1577–1640) – court painter, recently returned from Italy, and newly married – found himself in a position to buy a large house, where he lived and worked until his death. After centuries of neglect, the house was rescued by the City of Antwerp in 1937, and has been refurbished to look as it might have done in Rubens' day. Apart from the sheer charm of the place, it provides a rare opportunity to see the physical context in which great art was made.

Peter Paul Rubens

1 The Building
The house (above) is set around an inner courtyard. As you enter, the older, Flemish-style half is to the left – housing the domestic quarters, where Rubens lived. The right half, designed by the artist in grander Baroque style, contains his studio.

2 The Parlour
This room is notable for its wall hangings. Embossed Spanish leather was used as a kind of wall-paper in the houses of the well-to-do.

3 The Kitchen
This charming kitchen, with its tiled walls and open fireplace, is typical of Flanders. Note the pothooks with ratchets, designed to adjust the height of cooking vessels over the fire. The robust traditions of Flemish cuisine were forged in such kitchens.

4 The Baroque Portico
The massive ornamental screen was designed by Rubens in Italianate Baroque style to link the two parts of the house. It also provides a theatrical entrance to the formal garden beyond, with decorative elements.

The Dining Room 5
Eating and drinking played a central role in social habits of Rubens' day (right). A highlight in this room is a self-portrait of the artist, one of just four in existence.

6 The Art Gallery
A painting exhibited here, *The Art Gallery of Cornelis van der Geest* (above), shows how Rubens' own gallery might have looked – every inch of wall space hung with pictures.

7 The Little Bedroom

The most eye-catching item in this room is the 17th-century box bed in which people slept half sitting-up, said to promote good digestion.

Key to Floorplan
- Ground floor
- First floor

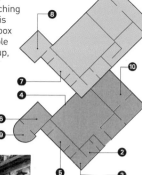

SWAGGER AND VERVE

Rubens began training as an artist aged 13, but it was an eight-year stay in Italy that transformed him. His work chimed with the grandeur and swagger of Baroque architecture and the Counter-Reformation, as well as with the luxurious lifestyle of the European aristocracy. Working with ceaseless energy, he and his dedicated assistants produced over 2,000 major paintings in his lifetime.

9 The Semi-Circular Museum

This elegant marble-lined room inspired by the Pantheon in Rome was used by Rubens to exhibit his collection of sculpture. Among the pieces shown today is a notable antique marble bust of Seneca.

10 Rubens' Studio

In this impressive room **(below)**, Rubens worked with a team of assistants and apprentices to maintain his huge productivity. Pictures shown here include the exhilarating but unfinished *Henry IV in the Battle of Ivry* (c.1628–30).

8 The Large Bedroom

This is the room in which Rubens died. The beautiful oak-and-ebony curio cabinet located here is decorated with mythological scenes based on Rubens' work.

NEED TO KNOW

MAP U2 ■ Wapper 9–11
■ 03 201 15 55
■ www.rubenshuis.be

Open 10am–5pm Tue–Sun. Closed Mon and public hols.

Adm: €8 (includes audio-guide; ID needed as security); those aged 12–25 and over 65 €6, under 12s free. Free on last Wed of every month

■ Next to the Rubenshuis is an elegant café-restaurant called Rubens Inn, serving snacks as well a substantial lunch menu. For a touch of modern style, the upbeat Grand Café Horta is just around the corner at Hopland 2 *(see p106)*.

■ The museum gets very busy at peak times, especially in summer. For some chance of a quieter visit, arrive at opening time – although you may find scores of other people have had the same idea.

TOP 10 ⭐ The Adoration of the Mystic Lamb, Ghent

St Bavo's cathedral in Ghent is home to one of Northern Europe's great cultural treasures. This huge, exquisitely painted polyptych is the masterpiece of brothers Hubrecht and Jan van Eyck. Its survival is a miracle. It was rescued from Protestant vandals in 1566, and from fire in 1822. Parts were taken by French soldiers in 1794, sold in 1816, then stolen in 1934. Undergoing a seven-year restoration, the polyptych is still on show but panels may be missing.

1 **The Polyptych**
The painting consists of 12 panels **(above)**, four in the centre and four on each of the folding wings. The lower tier depicts the spirituality of the world, and God's chosen people; the upper tier shows the heavenly realm, with Adam and Eve on either end.

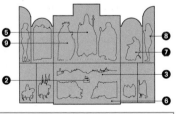

NEED TO KNOW

MAP Q2 ■ Sint-Baafskathedraal, Sint-Baafsplein ■ 09 269 20 45

Open Apr–Oct: 9:30am–5pm Mon–Sat, 1–5pm Sun; Nov–Mar: 10:30am–4pm Mon–Sat, 1–4pm Sun

Adm: €4, (7–12 yrs €1.50)

■ There are several friendly cafés immediately outside the cathedral. More spectacular, though, is the De Foyer café-restaurant on the first floor of the Schouwburg (theatre), with a terrace overlooking the square (see p113).

■ Get there well before closing time: the Vijd Chapel shuts promptly. Last tickets are issued 30 minutes before closing, including audioguides (which last 50 minutes).

5 God the Almighty

The central figure of the upper tier is God, depicted in a brilliant red robe and a bejewelled mitre (left), carrying a sceptre and with a crown at his feet. The benign calm and poise of the face radiate throughout the polyptych.

INFLUENCE ON EUROPEAN ART

Flemish painters are sometimes credited with inventing oil painting. This is an exaggeration, but certainly they perfected the technique. Antonello da Messina, the Italian credited with pioneering oil painting in Italy, is believed to have learnt his skills from Flemish artists. As a result of this, the advantages of oil painting over tempera or fresco became clear. Italian artists adopted oil painting, and Italian art accelerated toward the High Renaissance.

2 The Mystic Lamb of God

The focus of this panel (below) is the Lamb of God, which is spurting blood on an altar. It depicts four sets of figures approaching: virgin martyrs; figures from the New Testament and the Church; patriarchs and prophets of the Old Testament; and confessors of the Faith.

3 The Idealized City

To the rear of the central panel rise the towers and spires of the heavenly city of Jerusalem.

8 Eve

Jan van Eyck's contemporaries were startled by the realism of his Adam and Eve. Even today, their nudity among the luxuriously clothed figures is striking (left). They show the painter's great understanding of the human form.

4 The Inscription

In the 19th century, a verse inscription by the two brothers, thought to be original, was uncovered on the frame.

6 Flowers

The numerous flowers make a philosophical point: everything in nature is an expression of God's work. The painter's job was to record it faithfully.

9 Mary

The figure of Mary tells us much about the concept of feminine beauty in medieval times. Fine-featured, absorbed in her reading, she is decked with jewels.

7 The Angel-Musicians

A heavenly choir sings on one side of the upper tier (left), while on the other, an orchestra of angels plays. The figures are tightly crowded, but the perspective is good.

10 The External Panels

The wings of the painting can be closed. The external panels are tonally quite flat, intensifying the moment they are opened to reveal the sumptuous interior.

The Top 10
of Everything

**Beer on display at Huisbrouwerij
De Halve Maan, Bruges**

TOP 10 Moments in Belgian History

1 50s BC: Julius Caesar

The Roman army suffered repeated setbacks in its struggle against the courageous "Belgae", but Rome won out, and Belgium flourished under the Pax Romana of provincial rule for 400 years.

2 AD 843: Treaty of Verdun

After the Romans came the Franks, whose empire reached its apogee under Charlemagne. Following his death, his homeland was split by treaty along the River Scheldt – the division from which Flanders and Wallonia would evolve.

3 1302: Battle of the Golden Spurs

France dominated Flanders for much of the medieval period, resulting in popular revolt. At the Battle of the Golden Spurs, a Flemish rebel force humiliated the cream of the French army.

Battle of the Golden Spurs

4 1384: Burgundy Takes Over

When Louis de Male, Count of Flanders, died in 1384, his title was inherited by his son-in-law Philip the Bold (1342–1404), Duke of Burgundy. The dukes of Burgundy extended their control over the Low Countries. Burgundian rule reached a Golden Age under Philip the Good (reigned 1419–67). Bruges, his capital, was the centre of a rich trading empire.

5 1568: Religious Strife

Charles V, Holy Roman Emperor and King of Spain, inherited the Burgundian territories, but faced violent opposition as Protestantism gathered pace. A decisive moment came in 1568, during the reign of Philip II, when counts Egmont and Hoorn were executed in the Grand Place for opposing the persecution of Protestants. Eventually the territory was divided into Protestant north (the Netherlands) and Catholic south (now Belgium).

6 1815: Battle of Waterloo

When the Spanish Netherlands passed to Austria in 1713, conservative groups began to agitate for Belgian independence. Their revolt was swept aside in 1794 when the French revolutionary armies invaded. The Belgians were divided over the merits of Napoleonic rule, and fought on both sides when Napoleon was defeated by the Allies at Waterloo (see p69).

The Treaty of Verdun played a significant part in Belgian history

7 1830: The Belgian Revolution

Following Waterloo, the Congress of Vienna placed Belgium under Dutch rule, which was a deeply unpopular solution. Anger boiled over in 1830, independence was declared, and the Dutch army was forced out of Brussels.

Scenes from the Belgian Revolution

8 1914–18: World War I

At the outbreak of World War I, the German army swept into neutral Belgium. The Belgians thwarted their advance by flooding the land. The front settled near the medieval town of Ypres *(see p69)*. Over the next four years, half a million people from both sides died there.

9 1940–44: World War II

History was repeated in May 1940, when the German army launched a *Blitzkrieg* against neutral Belgium to outflank the Maginot Line, which blocked their entry into France. Brussels was liberated in September 1944.

10 1957: Treaty of Rome

Having been unwitting victims of two World Wars, the Belgians were enthusiastic supporters of the Treaty of Rome, which laid the foundations for the European Union. Over time, Brussels has effectively become the "Capital of Europe".

TOP 10 HISTORICAL FIGURES

1 Baldwin Iron-Arm
Baldwin (d. 878) became the first Count of Flanders, making Bruges his stronghold.

2 Pieter de Coninck and Jan Breydel
De Coninck, a weaver, and Breydel, a butcher, were instrumental in the successful Flemish rebellion against the French, launched in 1302.

3 Philip the Bold
Philip the Bold ushered in the Burgundian era in the Netherlands after inheriting control of Brussels and Flanders.

4 Philip the Good
Philip the Good founded the Order of the Golden Fleece and was a great patron of the arts.

5 Charles V
Born in Ghent, Charles V (1500–58) forged the largest empire in Europe since Roman times. His press is mixed.

6 Isabella and Albert
The dazzling court of the Infanta Isabella (1566–1633) and Archduke Albert (1559–1621) marked calmer times for Spanish Habsburg rule.

7 Charles of Lorraine
Austrian governor-general (ruled 1744–80) credited with bringing the Age of Enlightenment to Brussels.

8 King Léopold I
First King of the Belgians (ruled 1831–65), popular for his total commitment to the task.

9 King Léopold II
Second king of Belgium (ruled 1865–1909) *(see p84)*.

10 Paul-Henri Spaak
Socialist prime minister from 1938 to 1939 and during the post-war years, Spaak (1899–1972) played a central role in the creation of the European Community.

King Léopold I

ᴛᴏᴘ10 Famous Belgians

Hergé at work illustrating Tintin inside a copy of his famous comic book

1 Hergé

Georges Remi (1907–83) was a self-taught illustrator from the Brussels suburb of Etterbeek. In 1929 he published a story called *Tintin au Pays des Soviets*, and Belgium's most celebrated comic-strip character was born. Since then, 200 million Tintin books have been sold worldwide in some 50 languages. Georges Remi devised his pen name, Hergé, by simply reversing his initials and spelling out the sounds.

2 Georges Simenon

One of the world's best-selling authors, Simenon (1903–89) was born and bred in Liège. His most famous creation, which was Inspector Maigret, appeared in 75 of his 400 novels.

3 Gerard Mercator

Most school maps of the world are still based on the "Mercator projection" – an ingenious way of representing the spherical globe on a flat page. Mercator (1512–94) is also credited with creating the first "atlas", a word he introduced.

Gerard Mercator

4 Queen Astrid

Prince Léopold of Belgium married the beautiful Swedish princess Astrid in 1926. By the time of their coronation in 1934, they had three young children, but tragedy struck the following year when she was killed in a car accident in Switzerland, aged 29.

5 Jacques Brel

MAP C3 ■ Place de la Vieille Halle aux Blés 11, 1000 BRU ■ 02 511 10 20 ■ www.jacquesbrel.be ■ Open noon–6pm Tue–Sun; Aug: daily; closed Mon & public holidays ■ Adm

Jacques Brel (1929–78) still ranks in many people's minds as the greatest singer-songwriter in the French language. Although he first made his name in France, he remained loyal to his Belgian origins. The Jacques Brel Foundation in Brussels celebrates his life and work.

6 Johnny Hallyday

Although Johnny Hallyday (born 1943) is most famous as the "godfather of French rock 'n' roll", Belgium also claims him: his father was Belgian.

In a long career Hallyday has sold over 100 million records. He has also had a parallel career in film acting, impressing critics with his superb performance in the title role of *L'Homme du Train* (*The Man on the Train*, 2003).

7 Jean-Claude Van Damme

A former karate champion, Jean-Claude Van Damme (born 1960) did odd jobs in California, such as delivering pizzas and laying carpets, before making his name with action thrillers such as *Cyborg*, *Kickboxer* (1989) and *Universal Soldier* (1992).

8 Eddie Merckx

Cycling is a major sport in Belgium, and no name ranks higher than Eddie Merckx (born 1945), five times winner of the Tour de France (from 1969–72 and in 1974).

Eddie Merckx in action

9 Justine Henin

One of the great women tennis players of the early 2000s, famed for her athletic grace on the court, Henin (born 1982) won seven Grand Slam titles in her career. Her great Belgian rival Kim Clijsters won four.

10 Eden Hazard

One of a new generation of Belgian football stars, Hazard (born 1991) has played for Chelsea, Lille and Belgium. His compatriots on the international football stage include Romelu Lukaku, Vincent Kompany and Thibaut Courtois.

TOP 10 SLIGHTLY LESS-FAMOUS BELGIANS

Jacky Ickx, Formula One legend

1 Andreas Vesalius
Physician to Charles V and Philip II of Spain, Vesalius (1514–64) was known as "the father of modern anatomy".

2 Adolphe Sax
Best known as inventor of the saxophone, Sax (1814–94) devised a range of other musical instruments.

3 Father Damien
A missionary (1840–89) who devoted his life to caring for lepers in Hawaii. He was canonised in 2009 by Pope Benedict XVI.

4 Victor Horta
The innovative Art Nouveau architect credited with bringing the style to maturity *(see pp22–3)*.

5 Léo-Hendrik Baekeland
A great chemist (1863–1944) who invented Bakelite, the first totally synthetic plastic.

6 Henry van de Velde
Leading Art Nouveau designer (1863–1957) laid the foundations for the Bauhaus movement.

7 Jacky Ickx
Ickx was one of the great Formula One racing drivers of the 1960s and 1970s (born 1945).

8 Anne Teresa De Keersmaeker
A leading choreographer (born 1960) in the world of contemporary dance.

9 Dries van Noten
A celebrated fashion designer (born 1958) who has helped bring Antwerp to the forefront of *haute couture*.

10 Matthias Schoenaerts
Film actor and heart-throb (born 1977) who has achieved international acclaim in films including *Far from the Madding Crowd* (2015).

TOP 10 Belgian Artists

Altarpiece of the Seven Sacraments: Eucharist by Rogier van der Weyden

1 Jan van Eyck
The sheer technical brilliance and almost photographic detail of work by Jan van Eyck (c.1390–1441) are self-evident in paintings such as *Madonna with Canon Joris van der Paele (see p31)* and *The Adoration of the Mystic Lamb (see pp36–7)*. Van Eyck's work had a major impact on Italian art, and helped to fuel the Renaissance.

2 Rogier van der Weyden
Rogier van der Weyden (c.1400–64) was one of the leading Flemish "Primitives", and is best known for the intense emotion of his

Statue of van Eyck

work, such as *The Seven Sacraments* in the Koninklijk Museum voor Schone Kunsten, Antwerp *(see p101)*. Working mainly in Brussels, he became the leading painter after the death of van Eyck.

3 Hans Memling
Born in Germany, Hans Memling (c.1430–94) was probably trained by Rogier van der Weyden in Brussels before moving to Bruges. Memling went on to become one of the most successful artists of his day *(see pp30–31)*.

4 Pieter Bruegel the Elder
During the 16th century, Flemish artists turned to Italy for inspiration, which muddied their distinctive north European vision. But Pieter Bruegel (c.1525–69) rejected this trend and painted in a personal style based on what he saw around him. His depictions of rural villages generate a charm and honest naivety.

Rubens and Helene Fourment in the Garden (c. 1631), Rubens

5 Peter Paul Rubens
Almost all the best Flemish artists trained in Italy in the 16th century, and Peter Paul Rubens (1577–1640) used his experience to combine his prodigious Flemish technique with Italian flourish to produce art full of verve and dynamism.

6 Antoon van Dyck
Antoon van Dyck (1599–1641) was a colleague and friend of

Four Doctors of the Church, Jordaens

Rubens and matched many of the latter's skills, as well as addressing a similar range of subject matter. Van Dyck, however, is best known for his portraits. He became court painter to Charles I of England, who rewarded him with a knighthood.

7 Jacob Jordaens
After Rubens' death, another of his collaborators Jacob Jordaens (1593–1678) became Antwerp's leading painter, best remembered for allegorical paintings expressing the *joie-de-vivre* of the Baroque age.

8 James Ensor
The work of James Ensor (1860–1949) has earned him a reputation as one of art history's great eccentrics. His paintings incorporate skeletons, masks and hideous caricatures.

9 Paul Delvaux
Some memorable images of Surrealism came from the studio of Paul Delvaux (1897–1994). He is famous for his sensual, trance-like pictures of somnolent nudes in incongruous settings.

10 René Magritte
The dreamlike paintings of René Magritte (1898–1967) rank alongside Salvador Dalí's work as archetypal Surrealism. The Magritte Museum *(see p86)* displays paintings by the artist, plus photographs, drawings and archives.

TOP 10 LESSER-KNOWN BELGIAN ARTISTS

1 Constantin Meunier
Sculptor and painter (1831–1905) best-known for his bronzes of industrial workers *(see p85)*.

2 Émile Claus
Post-Impressionist painter (1849–1924) famous for rural scenes of sparkling clarity, achieved through a technique that he called "Luminism".

3 Jean Delville
One of the most inventive of the Symbolists (1867–1953), famed for colourful visions of Satanic forces.

4 Léon Frédéric
Symbolist (1856–1940) who combined social realism with poetic vision.

5 Fernand Khnopff
A painter (1858–1921) whose enigmatic Symbolist work is suffused with suppressed sexuality.

6 Léon Spilliaert
Symbolist (1881–1946) of great originality, whose works, often black and white, are instantly recognizable.

7 Rik Wouters
A painter and sculptor (1882–1916) whose work is noted for being full of light, verve and charm.

8 Constant Permeke
A painter (1886–1952) of the second phase of the Sint Martens Latem school. His work has a social edge and dark, gritty textures.

9 Panamarenko
True to Surrealist traditions, this artist (born 1940) creates machines and attempts to make them work.

10 Luc Tuymans
One of several contemporary Belgian artists who have achieved international recognition (born 1965).

Bords de la Lys (1920), Émile Claus

ᵀᴼᴾ **Churches**

Nave of Sint-Salvatorskathedraal, Bruges' majestic cathedral

1 Cathédrale des Saints Michel et Gudule, Brussels

Brussels' honey-coloured Gothic cathedral is a sanctuary of calm after the bustle of the Grand Place. Used for royal weddings and funerals *(see p74)*.

2 Église Saint-Jacques-sur-Coudenberg, Brussels

MAP D4 ▪ Place Royale, 1000 BRU (Ixelles) ▪ 02 511 78 36 ▪ Open noon–2pm Mon, noon–5:45pm Tue–Fri, 1–6pm Sat, 8:30am–6:45pm Sun

This distinctive church occupies a prominent position overlooking the Place Royale. Its bell tower apart, it looks more like a Roman temple than a Christian church.

3 Église Notre-Dame du Sablon, Brussels

The 15th-century church of the Guild of Crossbowmen is a beautiful example of Brabantine Gothic style, lit by large expanses of stained glass *(see p73)*.

4 Église Saint-Jean-Baptiste au Béguinage, Brussels

The lavish Flemish Baroque façade of this church contrasts with its history as the focal point of a *béguine* community of women *(see p75)*.

5 Sint-Salvators-kathedraal, Bruges

Both grand and sombre, the tone of this church befits its status as Bruges' cathedral. Although mainly Gothic, St Saviour's may date back in origin to early Christian times. The turreted tower was built in Neo-Medieval style in the late 19th century *(see p94)*.

6 Onze-Lieve-Vrouwekerk, Bruges

Bruges' most striking church, with a rocket-like spire in the austere style of Scheldt Gothic. The interior has been tinkered with ceaselessly since the 13th century. Its outstanding treasure is Michelangelo's *Madonna and Child*, donated by a wealthy merchant in 1514 *(see p92)*.

7 Sint-Jacobskerk, Antwerp

The richly ornate interior of this church bears testimony to the fact that it was frequented by the well-to-do during

Tomb, Sint-Jacobskerk

Antwerp's 17th-century heyday – among them was Rubens, who was buried in his family chapel here *(see p103)*.

8 Sint-Baafskathedraal, Ghent

The soaring Gothic interior and Baroque choir give Ghent's impressive cathedral a forceful quality *(see p109)*. It is upstaged, however, by its greatest treasure: Jan and Hubrecht van Eyck's magnificent *Adoration of the Mystic Lamb (see pp36–7)*.

9 Sint-Niklaaskerk, Ghent

The interior of Ghent's most attractive and imposing church has been scrubbed clean by a programme of restoration, resulting in a light and joyous space that makes the most of the robust Gothic stonework *(see p109)*.

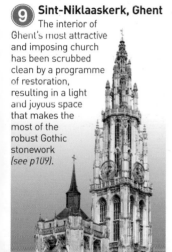

Onze-Lieve-Vrouwekathedraal

10 Onze-Lieve-Vrouwekathedraal, Antwerp

With one of its two towers unfinished, Antwerp's cathedral bears the battle scars of its centuries-long struggle for completion, but the immense interior gives an indication of the scale of its creators' ambitions. It's also an apt setting for two stunning triptychs by Rubens *(see pp32–3)*.

TOP 10 ARCHITECTURAL STYLES

A perfect example of Gothic style

1 Romanesque
10th–12th centuries. Semi-circular arches and hefty columns. The style is called "Norman" in Britain.

2 Gothic
13th–16th centuries. Pointed arches allowed for lighter structures.

3 Scheldt (or Scaldian) Gothic
13th–14th centuries. An early, rather austere version of Gothic typical of that found in northern Belgium (around the River Scheldt).

4 Brabantine and Flamboyant Gothic
14th–15th centuries. A daintier form of Gothic, which is used for town halls such as Bruges' Stadhuis.

5 Renaissance
15th–17th centuries. An elegant style taking its inspiration from Greek and Roman architecture.

6 Baroque
17th–18th centuries. A lavish interpretation of Classical style, full of exuberance and swagger.

7 Neo-Classical
18th–19th centuries. Classical revisited again, and even more determined to emulate Greek and Roman temples.

8 Neo-Gothic
19th-century. Gothic style revisited that was adopted particularly by the Catholic Revival.

9 Art Nouveau
Late 19th–early 20th centuries. A florid, organic style, an effort to create an utterly new approach: hence "new art".

10 Art Deco
1920s–1930s. A brash, angular but glamorous style. Name is based on a decorative arts exhibition in Paris 1925.

🔟 Art Nouveau Buildings in Brussels

Inside the Horta Museum

1 Horta Museum
The former home and studio of the great maestro of Art Nouveau architecture, Victor Horta, serves as a masterclass in the art *(see pp22–3)*.

2 Hôtel Tassel
Rue Paul-Émile Janson 6, 1050 BRU (Ixelles)

Designed by Victor Horta in 1893–5, this is considered the first Art Nouveau house. Up to this point, the well-to-do who commissioned new private mansions in the mushrooming Belgian suburbs adopted any style going, from Moorish to Medieval or Tuscan. Horta extrapolated from this "eclectic" style to evolve something more integrated and considered. The private mansion of a bachelor engineer, Hôtel Tassel was carefully tailored to all aspects of his lifestyle, but this individualized approach also made it less adaptable for subsequent owners.

3 Hôtel Saint-Cyr
Square Ambiorix 11, 1000 BRU (Brussels)

Art Nouveau tended toward excess, and this accusation is proven at this house – all loops and curves, with a circular picture window on the top floor. It was designed for painter Saint-Cyr in 1900.

4 Hôtel Hannon
MAP G2 ■ Avenue de la Jonction 1, 1060 BRU (Saint-Gilles)

Built in 1903–4, this was a private mansion designed by Jules Brunfaut for Édouard Hannon, an industrialist, painter and photographer with a keen interest in Art Nouveau. Access to the rare internal decorations is possible when the building is used to mount exhibitions.

5 La Maison Cauchie
Rue des Francs 5, 1040 BRU (Etterbeek) ■ 02 733 86 84 ■ Open 1st weekend of every month, 10am–1pm, 2–5:30pm ■ Adm

Behind a façade of geometric shapes with dreamy Art Nouveau murals lies the home of little-known painter Paul Cauchie (1875–1952).

6 Hôtel Ciamberlani
Rue Defacqz 48, 1050 BRU (Ixelles)

The artist Albert Ciamberlani (1864–1956) was one of those responsible for the huge mural in the triumphal colonnade of the Cinquantenaire

The façade of La Maison Cauchie

building *(see p51)*. He employed Paul Hankar (1859–1901), a key Art Nouveau architect, to build his house and studio in 1897. The façade combines iron, stone and brick for a highly individual decorative effect.

7 Musée des Instruments de Musique, Brussels

Art Nouveau was also called "Style Liberty", after the famous London store. Brussels' "Old England" store was named to echo this vogue. The building houses the Museum of Musical Instruments *(see pp20–21)*.

Wonderfully ornate Le Falstaff

8 Le Falstaff
MAP B3 ■ Rue Henri Maus 19, 1000 BRU (Brussels) ■ 02 511 57 59

This famous restaurant and drinking palace opposite the Bourse dates from 1903, and still powerfully evokes the era in which it was created. The interior is rich in Art Nouveau detail.

9 Comic Arts Museum

 Victor Horta designed the Magasins Waucquez, a textile shop, in 1903. Rescued in the 1970s, it has found new life as the famous comic-strip museum *(see pp26–7)*.

10 Hôtel Solvay
Avenue Louise 224, 1050 BRU (Ixelles)

The 33-year-old Victor Horta was still fairly unknown when he was commissioned to design this house by the industrialist Ernest Solvay. Its free-flowing form, with swirling wrought iron and a remarkably fluid use of stonework, established Horta as a master of the Art Nouveau style.

TOP 10 ARCHITECTURAL WONDERS

MAS, Antwerp

1 Jeruzalemkapel, Bruges
A Byzantine-influenced church inspired by a pilgrimage to the Holy Land *(see p95)*.

2 Palais de Justice, Brussels
Joseph Poelaert threw every Neo-Classical style in the book at this vast and domineering monument to justice *(see p76)*.

3 Pavillon Chinois, Tour Japonaise, Brussels
MAP G1 ■ Closed until further notice
Two beautiful oriental buildings rise up incongruously from the Parc de Laeken.

4 Serres Royales, Brussels
Magnificent royal greenhouses built in the 1870s *(see p86)*.

5 Hôtel Saint-Cyr, Brussels
Brussels' weirdest Art Nouveau building *(see opposite)*.

6 Centraal Station, Antwerp
Louis Delacenserie's station is a pot-pourri of Neo-Classical styles *(see p65)*.

7 The Palais Stoclet, Brussels
MAP H2 ■ Avenue de Tervuren 279, 1150 BRU (Woluwe Saint-Pierre)
Built 1905-11, with murals by Gustav Klimt, this radical private mansion was the architectural shocker of its day.

8 MAS, Antwerp
A striking and innovative museum, completed in 2011 *(see p102)*.

9 The Atomium, Brussels
A giant model of a crystal of iron, created for the 1958 Universal Exposition *(see p83)*.

10 Basilique Nationale du Sacré-Coeur, Brussels
There is something strangely soulless about this massive 20th-century church *(see p86)*.

📻🔟 Museums

1 Musées Royaux d'Art et d'Histoire, Brussels

Belgium's collection of historic national and international treasures is housed in this palatial building. It includes an impressive array of medieval church treasures (in the Salle aux Trésors), tapestries, Art Nouveau sculpture and jewellery, antique costumes and archaeological finds. One of three museums in the Parc du Cinquantenaire (see p84).

Treasures at Musée Charlier, Brussels

2 Musée des Instruments de Musique, Brussels

Housed in a classic Art Nouveau department store, perched on a ridge, "Le mim" is one of Brussels' must-see sights. More than 1,200 multifarious exhibits are enhanced by listening to their sounds on an iPad-like device (see pp20–21).

3 Volkskundemuseum, Bruges

See life as it was lived by the ordinary folk of Bruges in the often threadbare 19th and early 20th centuries. Fascinating collections of household items, as well as complete workshops, bring home the extraordinary changes of the last century and a half (see p95).

4 Musée Charlier, Brussels

A rare opportunity to see inside one of Brussels' maisons de maître (mansions). As well as a fine collection of antique furniture, the Hôtel Charlier contains many reminders of its days as a meeting place for the avant-garde set in the early 20th century (see p74).

5 Museum Aan de Stroom (MAS), Antwerp

This dynamic construction of perspex and red sandstone is packed with ethnographic and folkloric treasures – plus there are great city views from the rooftop (see p102).

An exhibit at Museum Aan de Stroom, Antwerp

6 Gruuthusemuseum, Bruges

For over 100 years this historic house has served as a museum presenting an ever-growing collection of artifacts from daily life – both lowly and grand – dating from Bruges' medieval Golden Age to the 19th century. The museum is currently closed for restoration until the end of 2017 (see p93).

Folk artifacts at Volkskundemuseum

THE CINQUANTENAIRE

Parc du Cinquantenaire arch

The era of great international fairs was launched by the Great Exhibition in Hyde Park, London, in 1851. King Léopold II decided to mount a similar exhibition to mark the 50th anniversary *(cinquantenaire)* of the founding of Belgium in 1880. The site chosen was marshland to the east of the historic centre of Brussels. A pair of exhibition complexes, linked by a monumental semi-circular colonnade, was commissioned from Gédéon Bordiau. The project was not completed in time for the 1880 jubilee, but building continued, and the site was used for subsequent fairs. The central triumphal arch – topped by a quadriga reminiscent of the one on Berlin's Brandenburg Gate – was completed in 1905 to mark Belgium's 75th anniversary. Bordiau's barrel-vaulted exhibition hall houses the Musée Royal de l'Armée et d'Histoire Militaire. Its twin to the south was destroyed by fire in 1946; its replacement now forms part of the Musées Royaux d'Art et d'Histoire. The Parc and Palais du Cinquantenaire also contain Autoworld *(see p84)*, as well as two curiosities: the Atelier de Moulage and the Pavillon Horta-Lambeaux *(see p84)*.

7 Horta Museum, Brussels

The full artistic potential of Art Nouveau is apparent in this museum – formerly the house and offices of Victor Horta, the father of Art Nouveau architecture *(see pp22–3)*.

8 Design Museum Gent, Ghent

Anyone interested in antique furniture and the history of the decorative arts will love this delightful museum, which follows changing styles from the domestic elegance of the 17th century to the jocular irreverence of Milanese Post-Modernism *(see p111)*.

9 Huis van Alijn, Ghent

This folk museum, set out in almshouses founded by the Alijn family in the 14th century, is a major repository for a huge range of artifacts that were part and parcel of the lives of ordinary Flemish people in past centuries *(see p110)*.

Museum Plantin-Moretus, Antwerp

10 Museum Plantin-Moretus, Antwerp

Within a century of Gutenberg's breakthrough in European printing by means of movable type, this 16th-century printing house (now a UNESCO World Heritage Site) had become a leader of the publishing revolution. Visitors can view historic printing presses and engraving plates in the workshop *(see p102)*.

TOP10 Art Galleries

The Village Lawyer (1621) by Pieter Brueghel the Youger at MSK, Ghent

1 Museum voor Schone Kunsten (MSK), Ghent

Ghent's museum of fine arts is a bit of a mixed bag, but has a handful of outstanding pieces; just a stone's throw from SMAK *(see p111)*.

2 Musée d'Ixelles, Brussels

This small but rewarding collection of art boasts names such as Rembrandt, Toulouse-Lautrec and Picasso, as well as leading Belgian artists such as Léon Spilliaert. The museum is located in Ixelles, south of the city centre *(see p84)*.

3 Koninklijk Museum voor Schone Kunsten (KMSKA), Antwerp

One of the great European collections, but closed for restoration until the end of 2018. In the meantime, key elements are being shown in various places around the city in temporary exhibitions *(see p101)*.

4 Musées Royaux des Beaux-Arts, Brussels

Brussels' royal museum of fine art holds rich collections of such artists as Bruegel, Rubens and Jordaens. Outstanding 19th-century art and Art Nouveau is shown in the separate but integrated Fin-de-Siècle Museum, and the Magritte Museum next door has a comprehensive collection of the great Surrealist's work *(see pp18–19)*.

5 Meunier Museum, Brussels

The suburban home of the late-19th-century sculptor Constantin Meunier has been turned into a gallery devoted to his work; it leaves visitors in no doubt of his gifts and the pungency of his social criticism *(see p85)*.

6 Van Buuren Museum, Brussels

A private collection of art is presented in its original setting: a charming Art Deco home with a beautiful garden *(see p83)*.

Koninklijk Museum, Antwerp

7 Groeningemuseum, Bruges

Bruges' main gallery is celebrated for its collection of paintings by Flemish Masters of the late medieval "Golden Age". A small, easily digestible museum *(see pp30–31).*

8 Sint-Janshospitaal, Bruges

A superb collection of paintings by Flemish Primitive Hans Memling was originally commissioned for the chapel of this medieval hospital to bring solace to the sick. The conjoining wards and chapel have been restored, giving these works a fascinating context *(see pp30–31).*

9 Stedelijk Museum voor Actuele Kunst (SMAK), Ghent

This acclaimed gallery of contemporary art not only mounts cutting-edge temporary exhibitions, but also has a remarkable permanent collection. The works on display are guaranteed to provoke a reaction from aficionados and the unconverted alike *(see p111).*

MUHKA, Antwerp

10 Museum van Hedendaagse Kunst (MUHKA), Antwerp

The location of this contemporary art gallery, in the up-and-coming former dockland area in the south of the city, sets the tone for what lies inside. A ground-breaking museum *(see p104).*

TOP 10 WORKS OUTSIDE GALLERIES

A replica of Rodin's *The Thinker*

1 The Adoration of the Mystic Lamb (1432)
Jan and Hubrecht van Eyck's masterpiece *(see pp36–7).*

2 The Raising of the Cross (1609–10)
Wonderful triptych by Pieter Paul Rubens *(see p34).*

3 The Descent from the Cross (1611–14)
Rubens' triptych contrasts Christ's death with the Nativity *(see p34).*

4 Madonna and Child (1504–5)
Michelangelo sculpture of mesmeric dignity *(see p92).*

5 Baroque Pulpit (1699)
Hendrik Verbruggen's elaborate carved pulpit in Brussels' cathedral *(see pp74–5).*

6 The History of Bruges (1895)
In the Stadhuis of Bruges *(see pp28–9),* 12 superb Neo-Medievalist murals by Albert and Julien De Vriendt.

7 The Thinker (c.1905)
MAP F1 ■ Parvis Notre-Dame, 1020 BRU (Laeken) ■ Open 8:30am–4:30pm daily
A copy of Rodin's statue on a tomb in Laeken Cemetery, Brussels.

8 Hergé Mural (1983)
MAP H2 ■ Stockel Metro, Brussels
A cartoon mural decorating Stockel metro station by Hergé.

9 Fountain of Kneeling Youths (1898)
Emile Braunplein (in front of the Belfort, Ghent)
George Minne's best-known work.

10 Nos Vieux Trams Bruxellois (1978)
Bourse Station, Brussels
Paul Delvaux's contribution to putting art in the metro.

🔟 Off the Beaten Track

Église St-Jean-Baptiste au Béguinage, Brussels

1 Église St-Jean-Baptiste au Béguinage, Brussels

This understated Baroque church was once at the heart of an extensive *béguinage (see box p92)*, and still provides tranquillity for visitors close to the heart of the city *(see p75)*.

2 Librarium, Royal Library of Belgium, Brussels

MAP C4 ■ 02 519 53 11
■ www.kbr.be/librarium
■ Open 9am–5pm Mon–Sat

In a softly lit, darkened space in Belgium's most august library is a small and charming museum devoted to books, writing and libraries. Fascinating exhibits, and the preserved writing-rooms and libraries of authors and collectors, are augmented by temporary exhibitions. (Entrances on Mont des Arts and Boulevard de l'Empereur 2.)

3 Maison Autrique, Brussels

This large and grand private mansion, in the northern suburb of Schaerbeek, was designed by Victor Horta in 1893. It was his first project, just before he really embraced the Art Nouveau style. The mansion, from the cellar kitchen to the attic, has been restored and furnished in original style so that visitors can view the furnishings and decor of late 19th-century life *(see p86)*.

4 Van Buuren Museum, Brussels

Head out to the southern suburb of Uccle to find the comfortable 1920s Art Deco home and gardens of David and Alice van Buuren. They surrounded themselves with a superb collection of art by many of the leading Belgian and European artists, both historic and contemporary *(see p83)*.

5 Patershol, Ghent

MAP Q1

Behind the Huis van Alijn folk museum *(see p110)* is a warren of cobbled streets, once the heart of medieval Ghent and home to leatherworkers and Carmelite Friars (Paters). In the 17th and 18th centuries, magistrates working at the nearby fortress, the Gravensteen, lived here, which accounts for some of the grander houses, but during Ghent's industrialisation in the 19th century the area became a notorious slum. Restoration began in the 1980s and the Patershol has now been pedestrianized and gentrified, but it still retains an authentic charm.

Charming Patershol district, Ghent

6 Eastern Bruges

Most visitors to Bruges frequent the centre and southwest of the city. Head east for peace and quiet, and a collection of interesting churches and museums *(see p95)*.

Galerie Bortier, Brussels

7 Galerie Bortier, Brussels

Time stands still among the second-hand books and prints on sale beneath the glass canopies of this 1847 shopping arcade *(see p77)*.

8 Maison d'Érasme and Béguinage d'Anderlecht, Brussels

These two enchanting museums, in the western suburb of Anderlecht, are close enough together to be visited in a single trip *(see p86)*.

9 Muur der Dood-geschotenen, Bruges
MAP M3

At the site of a former barracks on the Kazernevest, in eastern Bruges, a bullet-marked brick wall and a line of monuments commemorates the place where a dozen men were executed by the German army during World War I. The one British victim was Captain Fryatt, a merchant navy officer, whose death became a *cause célèbre* at the time.

10 Begijnhof, Antwerp
MAP U1 ■ Rodestraat 39 ■ 03 232 01 03 ■ Open 8am–6pm daily

A place of therapeutic calm, Antwerp's *béguinage* (*begijnhof* in Dutch) was built originally in 1545, and is still used as housing.

TOP 10 BEST PARKS AND OPEN SPACES

1 Parc de Bruxelles (Warande)
MAP D3
Lovely formal park laid out in the 18th century, in front of the Palais Royal.

2 Place du Petit Sablon, Brussels
A tiny park famous for its statues of medieval guildworkers on the railings *(see p73)*.

3 Parc d'Egmont, Brussels
MAP C5
A green oasis close to the Avenue Louise shopping hub.

4 Étangs d'Ixelles, Brussels
MAP G2
Two large ponds, good for a stroll or a picnic when visiting the Horta Museum and the Art Nouveau district.

5 Forêt de Soignes, Brussels
The great beech forest to the south of the city *(see p68)*.

6 Minnewater, Bruges
The so-called "Lake of Love", with surrounding park, in the south of Bruges *(see p94)*.

7 Koningin Astridpark, Bruges
MAP L4
An agreeable park, with children's play equipment, featured in the 2008 film *In Bruges*.

8 Citadelpark, Ghent
MAP P6
A great park with Ghent's main art galleries; on the city's eastern edge.

9 Stadspark, Antwerp
MAP U3
A triangular lung, southeast of the centre of Antwerp.

10 Middelheim Museum, Antwerp
A rewarding open-air sculpture park *(see p104)*.

Minnewater in autumn, Bruges

⟨TOP 10⟩ Children's Attractions

Visitors enjoying the penguin enclosure at Antwerp Zoo

1 Antwerp Zoo
MAP V2 ■ Koningin
Astridplein 26 ■ 03 202 45 40
■ www.zooantwerpen.be ■ Open
10am–late afternoon daily (closing
times vary between 4:45 & 7pm)
■ Adm
One of the oldest zoos in the world
(1843). Special attractions include
a sea lion show, elephant bathing,
a hippo pond and a hands-on reptile
experience. The zoo is also a Centre
for Research and Conservation.

2 Bruparck, Brussels
MAP F1 ■ Bvd du Centenaire
20, 1020 BRU ■ 02 474 83 83
■ www.bruparck.com ■ Opening
hours vary; check in advance ■ Adm
Near the Atomium (see p82) is an
amusement park to entertain all
the family – with a cinema,
swimming-pool and
"Mini-Europe".

3 Comics Art Museum, Brussels
Older children will
be intrigued by this
unusual museum;
younger children
may not be, especially
if they speak neither
French nor Dutch
(see pp26–7).

**Snowy, Comics
Art Museum**

4 Historic Tram Ride, Brussels
This fun tram ride should appeal
to children of all ages. A vintage
tram strains and squeaks its way
along a 40-km (25-mile) circuit
of wooded paths from the Musée
du Tram (see p86). It operates on
Sundays from April to September.

5 Musée du Jouet, Brussels
Toy museums have a habit of boring
children stiff, but this one bucks the
trend with its welcoming atmosphere
and hands-on exhibits (see p76).

6 Mannekin-Pis Costume Collection, Brussels
You may be lucky to find the
Mannekin-Pis (see p16) on
one of his dressed-up
days. In any case, it's
always fun to see his
wardrobe in the Maison
du Roi (see p15), where
about 100 of his 815
outfits are on display.

7 Belfort, Bruges
A kind of medieval
theme-park experience:
the physical challenge of
a slightly scary spiral
staircase, magnificent
views from the top, and a

bit of a shock if the bells ring while you are up there. There may be a queue to get in (see p91).

8 Walibi Belgium

Wavre ■ Walibi Belgium: 010 42 15 00. Aqualibi: 010 42 16 03 ■ **Opening times vary; see website for details** ■ **www.walibi.com** ■ **Adm**

Belgium's premier amusement park, with everything from scary roller coasters and vertical drops to soak-to-the-skin water rides, plus more gentle, traditional tracked car-rides and roundabouts for younger visitors. There is also a multi-pool swimming complex, called Aqualibi, with a host of shoots and tube-runs.

Boat trip on a canal in Bruges

9 Canal Boat Trips, Bruges and Ghent

From a canal boat the landmarks of Bruges and Ghent show themselves in a new light. Boats leave from various spots in the centre of Bruges and from the Graslei and Korenlei in Ghent (see p109).

10 Boudewijn Seapark, Bruges

Alfons De Baeckestraat 12, 8200 Sint-Michiels ■ 050 38 38 38 ■ **www. boudewijnseapark.be** ■ **Opening times vary; check in advance** ■ **Adm**

Bruges' amusement park, in a suburb to the south of the city, features marine-themed rides and attractions, such as an orca-themed roller coaster and an aqua park with slides and water fountains.

TOP 10 OTHER SIGHTS FOR CHILDREN

1 Parc du Cinquantenaire, Brussels
The three major museums in this park will appeal to all ages (see p84).

2 mim, Brussels
Music in the headphones changes as you go around – a winning formula (see pp20–21).

3 Muséum des Sciences Naturelles, Brussels
Good for the scientist, ecologist and dinosaur fanatic (see p86).

4 Musée des Enfants, Brussels
Rue du Bourgmestre 15, 1050 BRU (Ixelles) ■ 02 640 01 07
Popular museum for children aged 4–12. Limited numbers.

5 Choco-Story, Brussels
MAP B3 ■ Rue de la Téte d'Or 9–11, 1000 BRU ■ 02 514 20 48 ■ www. choco-story-brussels.be ■ Open 10am–5pm daily (last entry 4:30pm) ■ Adm
See and taste chocolate in the making.

6 Huis van Alijn, Ghent
Magical folk museum (see p110).

7 Het Gravensteen, Ghent
MAP P1 ■ Sint-Veerleplein ■ 09 225 93 06
This heavily restored medieval castle is complete with dungeons.

8 Waterloo, Brussels
The battlefield has a visitor centre and various outlying museums (see p69).

9 Historium, Bruges
Multi-media history of medieval Bruges (see p94).

10 Aquatopia, Antwerp
MAP V2 ■ Koningin Astridplein 7 ■ 03 205 07 50 ■ www.aquatopia.be ■ 10am–6pm daily ■ Adm
This lively aquarium stands opposite Centraal station.

Het Gravensteen, Ghent

TOP 10 **Performing Arts Venues**

high-profile acts. The largest of the three concert halls has a capacity of 2,000.

Théâtre Royal de la Monnaie, Brussels

1 Théâtre Royal de la Monnaie, Brussels

MAP C2 ■ Place de la Monnaie, 1000 BRU ■ 070 23 39 39 ■ www.lamonnaie.be

The most revered performing arts venue in the country, La Monnaie (Dutch: De Munt) is celebrated for sparking off the Revolution of 1830 (see p41), when a crowd took to the streets incited by Auber's opera La Muette de Portici. It was rebuilt in Neo-Classical style in 1819; the interior was redesigned after a fire in 1855.

2 Palais des Beaux-Arts, Brussels (BOZAR)

MAP D4 ■ Rue Ravenstein 23, 1000 BRU ■ 02 507 82 00 ■ www.bozar.be

Victor Horta's Palais des Beaux-Arts was completed in 1928. Known as BOZAR, it is a multi-arts venue, covering music, theatre and more.

3 Ancienne Belgique, Brussels

MAP B3 ■ Boulevard Anspach 110, 1000 BRU ■ 02 548 24 84 ■ www.abconcerts.be

This well-established venue for pop and rock concerts, in central Brussels, presents interesting and

4 Les Halles de Schaerbeek, Brussels

MAP G2 ■ Rue Royale Sainte-Marie 22a, 1030 BRU (Schaerbeek) ■ 02 218 21 07 ■ www.halles.be

The magnificent old covered market, built in iron and glass at the end of the 19th century, has been transformed into an inspirational venue for a variety of cultural events – including drama, dance and music.

5 Concertgebouw, Bruges

MAP J5 ■ 't Zand 34 ■ 070 22 33 02 ■ www.concertgebouw.be

As part of its celebrations as the Cultural Capital of Europe in 2002, Bruges created a new concert hall. The result is a highly innovative building that quickly became established as a leading venue for classical music, as well as ballet and jazz.

Théâtre Royal de Toone

6 Théâtre Royal de Toone, Brussels

MAP C3 ■ Rue du Marché aux Herbes 66 (Impasse Sainte Pétronille), 1000 BRU ■ 02 511 71 37 ■ www.toone.be

The Toone marionette theatre, occupying a tiny building at the bottom of a medieval alley, is a Brussels institution. Note that this is not for children: the plays – enacted by traditional puppets made of wood and papier-mâché – may be serious classics of theatre, and the language is often Bruxellois, the rich dialect of the city. You can also visit the museum of retired puppets.

De Vlaamse Opera, Ghent
MAP Q3 ■ Schouwburgstraat 3
■ 070 22 02 02 ■ www.operaballet.be
Ghent home of the much-respected Vlaamse Opera, this classic opera house ranks among the most spectacular theatres in Europe.

8 De Vlaamse Opera, Antwerp
MAP U2 ■ Frankrijklei 3 ■ 070 22 02 02 ■ www.operaballet.be
Antwerp's opera house was completed in 1907, with its interior elegantly decked out with marble and gilding. The Vlaamse Opera also performs here.

Le Botanique, Brussels

Le Botanique, Brussels
MAP D1 ■ Rue Royale 236, 1210 BRU (Saint-Josse-ten-Noode)
■ 02 218 37 32 ■ www.botanique.be
The beautiful glasshouses of Brussels' botanical gardens were built in 1826–9. Cunning conversion of the interior has provided what is now a key venue for a wide range of cultural activities, including theatre, dance and concerts of all kinds.

deSingel, Antwerp
Desguinlei 25 ■ 03 248 28 28 ■ www.desingel.be
This vibrant multi-purpose cultural centre is a venue for performances and exhibitions of drama, dance, architecture and music.

TOP 10 BELGIAN WRITERS, POETS AND MUSICIANS

Django Reinhardt and his band

1 Roland de Lassus
Also known as Orlando di Lasso (c.1532–94). One of the leading composers of his day.

2 César Franck
Organist and composer (1822–90) in the Romantic tradition.

3 Émile Verhaeren
Symbolist poet (1855–1916) noted for his portrayals (in French) of Flanders.

4 Maurice Maeterlinck
Nobel-Prize-winning Symbolist poet and dramatist (1862–1949).

5 Michel de Ghelderode
Belgium's most celebrated 20th-century playwright (1898–1962), and one of the most original writers in the French language.

6 Georges Simenon
Prolific master of the popular detective story (1903–89) and creator of Inspector Maigret (see p42).

7 Django Reinhardt
The most celebrated of all jazz guitarists, Reinhardt (1910–53) was a key member of the renowned Quintet of the Hot Club of France.

8 Arthur Grumiaux
A leading violinist of his era (1921–86).

9 Hugo Claus
Among Belgium's most revered writers (1929–2008) is this Bruges-born poet, playwright and novelist.

10 Amélie Nothomb
One of Belgium's most successful modern novelists (born 1967), noted for her exploration of the darker sides of human nature.

🔟 Types of Belgian Beer

1 Witbier/Bière Blanche
Most beer is made from barley, but it can also be made from wheat to produce a distinctive "white beer" to which flavourings such as coriander and orange peel may be added. The result is a light, sparkling and refreshing beer, often served cloudy with sediment. Examples include Hoegaarden and Brugs.

2 Kriek
Lambic (see opposite page) can be flavoured with cherries (formerly the cherries of the north Brussels orchards of Schaerbeek), added during fermentation to create a highly distinctive drink called *kriek*. With raspberries it makes *framboise*; with candy sugar it makes *faro*. Of the three, newcomers may find *faro* the easiest to begin with.

3 Strong Ales
Some breweries pride themselves on the sheer power of their product. Duvel ("Devil"), at 8.5%, is a famous example. Several lay claim to being the strongest beer in Belgium; at 12%, Bush is a contender, and to be treated with respect.

4 Trappist Beer
In the past, some of Belgium's finest beers were made by the Trappists, a silent order of Cistercian monks. Now it's produced commercially by six breweries with close ties to the monasteries (Chimay, Achel, Westmalle, Orval, Rochefort and Westvleteren). Yeast is added at bottling to induce a second fermentation; it is important to pour off carefully in one go to avoid disturbing the sediment.

A bottle of *kriek*

5 Abbey Beer
Other abbeys also produced beer but, unlike the Trappist monasteries, many have licensed them to commercial breweries. Leffe, for example, is now owned by AB InBev. That said, many of the abbey beers are excellent. In addition, there are good "abbey-style" beers, such as Ename, Floreffe and St Feuillien.

6 Double/Triple
Traditionally, breweries graded their beers by strength: apparently single was around 3%, double 6% and triple 9%. Some breweries – notably the Abbeys – still label their beers double *(dubbel)* and triple *(tripel)*. Double is usually a dark and sweetish brew, triple often golden-blond.

7 Lager-Style Beers
Pils, or lager, is a bottom-fermented beer: the yeast remains at the bottom of the brew (stronger,

Orval Abbey, famous for its Trappist beer produced by the monks

heavier ales tend to be top-fermented, which seals in more flavour). Although such light beers may be sniffed at by connoisseurs in other countries, in Belgium they are brewed to a high standard. Despite its ubiquity, AB InBev's famous Stella Artois, brewed in Leuven, is a good-quality lager.

Barrels of fermenting beer, Lambic

8 Lambic

In the valley of the Senne, the river that flows through Brussels, there is a natural air-borne yeast called *Brettanomyces*. For centuries, brewers have simply left their warm wheat-beer wort uncovered during the winter months, and allowed air to deliver the yeast into it. The fermenting beer is then left to mature in wooden casks for a year or more. This creates a very distinctive beer, with a slightly winey edge, called *lambic* – the quint-essential beer of Brussels.

9 Gueuze

Lambic of various ages can be blended, and then fermented a second time in the bottle. This produces a beer called *gueuze*, which is fizzy like champagne and matured a further year or two to accentuate the wine-like qualities of the original product.

10 Christmas Beers

Many of the breweries produce Christmas ales for the festive season. These may just be prettily labelled versions of their usual brew, but they may also be enriched ales of high strength.

TOP 10 CLASSIC BELGIAN DISHES

1 Carbonnades Flamandes/Vlaamse Stoverij
A beef stew cooked in Belgian beer – rich, succulent and sweet, and best eaten with *frites* and mayonnaise.

2 Moules marinière
Mussels, steamed until they open, in white wine flavoured with celery, onion and parsley; usually served in something resembling a bucket, accompanied by a plate of *frites*.

3 Waterzooi
A creamy, comforting dish of chicken (or fish) with vegetables in broth; a traditional dish of Ghent.

4 Chicons au Gratin
Belgian endives wrapped in ham and baked in a creamy cheese sauce.

5 Anguilles au Vert/Paling in 't Groen
Eels cooked in a thick sauce of fresh green herbs.

6 Garnaalkroketten
Deep-fried potato croquettes filled with fresh shrimps; they make an excellent starter or snack.

7 Salade Liégeoise
A warm salad of potatoes and green beans, or *salade frisée*, with fried bacon bits.

8 Stoemp
Mashed potato mixed with a vegetable, such as carrots, leeks or celeriac.

9 Flamiche aux Poireaux
A quiche-like tart, made with leeks.

10 Jets d'Houblon
Hop-shoots – a spring-time by-product of brewing – usually served in a cream sauce. They taste a bit like asparagus.

Moules marinière

🔟 Things to Buy

Antiques and bric-à-brac for sale at Stefantiek in Brussels

1 Antiques and Bric-à-brac

For lovers of everything from old comics and Art Nouveau door handles to exquisite Louis XVI desks and ormolu clocks, Belgium is a happy hunting ground. In Brussels, the full range is on view between the Place du Jeu de Balle and the Place du Grand Sablon (see p77).

2 Chocolate

Belgian chocolate is justly famous for its smooth, delicious taste. The manufacturers use high-quality cocoa beans and reintroduce a generous proportion of cocoa butter. They also invented the means to manufacture filled chocolates (or pralines) on an industrial scale. As a result, these superb chocolates are remarkably good value.

3 Beer

In 1900 there were over 3,200 breweries in Belgium; now there are just over 150, but they still generate an astonishing variety of beers (see pp60–61). The most famous, and also some of the finest, are produced by the Trappist monasteries, but even the lighter, lager-style beers such as Stella Artois and Jupiler are made to a high standard. There are specialist beer shops in all the main cities.

4 Biscuits and Pâtisserie

It is hard not to drool in front of the ravishing shop windows of Belgian pâtisseries – and the mouth-watering offerings usually taste as good as they look. An alternative is to buy some of the equally famed biscuits – from a specialist such as Dandoy (see p17).

5 Tapestry

Tapestry was one of the great medieval industries of Brussels and Bruges. It is still made on a craft basis, but of course large pieces come at luxury prices.

6 Haute Couture

Since the 1980s, Belgium has shot to the forefront of the fashion world, with designers such as Dries van Noten, Raf Simons and Walter van Beirendonck. Many of the major

Exquisite Belgian handmade lace

designers have their own shops in Antwerp (see p105), but there are plenty of outlets in the Rue Antoine Dansaert in Brussels (see p77).

7 Lace

There were tens of thousands of lace-makers in 19th-century Belgium, many of them living in penury. That industry was undermined by the invention of lace-making machines, and to some degree it still is. If you want to buy handmade Belgian lace, go to a reputable shop, insist on a label of authenticity, and expect a high price.

8 Children's Clothes

There are numerous shops devoted to children's clothes in Belgium, and their products are irresistible – from hard-wearing romp-around cottons to beautifully made winter jackets and hats, and unusual, fun shoes.

9 Tintin Merchandise

Tintin fans can pick up not only the books, but also T-shirts, figurines, games, post-cards, mobile phone covers, key rings, stationery, mugs – you name it. The characters are copyrighted, so high-quality, legally produced goods come at a fairly steep price. There is a dedicated Tintin shop in Rue de la Colline, Brussels.

Tintin figure

10 Diamonds

HRD: www.hrdantwerp.com

Over three-quarters of the world's uncut diamonds flow through the exchanges of Antwerp; many of these are cut, polished and mounted there. You could find some bargains – but of course, you have to know what you're doing. If in doubt, consult the Hoge Raad voor Diamant (HRD), which oversees a reliable system of certification.

TOP 10 SUPPLIERS OF CHOCOLATES, BISCUITS AND PÂTISSERIE

Chocolate strawberries at Godiva

1 Leonidas
www.leonidas.com
One of the favourite chocolatiers. Less rich and less expensive than its rivals.

2 Godiva
www.godivachocolates.eu
Maker of luxury chocs, with branches not just in Belgium but worldwide.

3 Neuhaus
www.neuhaus.be
Credited with inventing the praline and the *ballotin* (box).

4 Dumon
www.chocolatierdumon.be
Excellent chocolatier originating from Torhout, near Bruges: a cut above the mass-market producers.

5 Wittamer
www.wittamer.com
Chocolates, cakes and biscuits to die for (see p78).

6 Pierre Marcolini
www.marcolini.be
Fabulous chocolates, made entirely from raw ingredients.

7 Mary
www.mary.be
Chocolates of exquisite quality.

8 Galler
A mass-market but high-standard manufacturer. Its famous Langues de Chat (cat's tongues) are shaped in a jokey cat's face.

9 Maison Dandoy
Supreme biscuit manufacturer, in a class of its own.

10 Jules Destrooper
www.destrooper.be
Manufacturer of biscuits since 1886. Its distinctive blue-and-white boxes contain such delights as "almond thins".

TOP 10 Brussels, Bruges, Antwerp & Ghent for Free

1 Grand Place, Brussels
The spectacular centrepiece of Brussels is a marvel of ornate architecture. There are a couple of attractions with entrance charges to visit here, but the best is free: standing in the middle looking at the façades in wonder *(see pp14–15)*.

2 Manneken-Pis, Brussels
On view in all his unashamed glory, just a short walk from the Grand Place, is Brussels' most famous and notorious mascot *(see p73)*. Access to the statue is free, but you will have to pay to see his collection of costumes at the Maison du Roi *(see p15)*, unless you go on the first Sunday of the month.

3 Africa Museum
Although the Africa Museum in Tervuren is currently closed, its beautifully landscaped gardens are open and free of charge. You can saunter past monumental geometric topiary and stunning Neo-Classical fountains, picnic near the neatly laid out lakes and stroll through ancient woodland. And, if you are lucky, you might be there when the museum opens for one of its free weekend pop-up exhibitions.

4 Parlement Européen and the Parlementarium, Brussels
For all avid political enthusiasts here's a chance to see what goes on at the EU Parliament and get an insight into the lives and work of MEPs – and all for free *(see p84)*.

The Maagdenhuismuseum, Antwerp

5 Museums: free entry days
Many of the publicly owned museums offer free entry one day a month. For example, on the first Wednesday each month, after 1pm, there is no charge at the Musées Royaux des Beaux-Arts *(see pp18–19)* and the Musée des Instruments de Musique *(see pp20–21)* in Brussels. Most public museums in Antwerp are also free on the first Wednesday of the month; the Maagdenhuismuseum *(see p104)* and the Rubenshuis *(see p36)* on the last.

6 Graslei and Korenlei, Ghent
These two historic quays, facing each other over the River Leie, are joined by a bridge, the Sint-Michielsbrug. This provides an excellent viewpoint, taking in both quays and the towers of the Sint-Niklaaskerk, the Belfort and Sint-Baafskathedraal *(see p109)*.

Graslei Quay

7 Walking in Bruges

One of the best things to do in Bruges is simply to walk. Bring stout shoes (for the cobbles) and wander. Virtually every sector of the city within the ovoid perimeter – formed by canals and roads that track the path of the old city walls – yields something of interest. Many hotels will supply maps with walks marked on them.

8 Centraal Station, Antwerp

MAP V2

This is a classic monument to the Golden Age of railways; a station of palatial richness, referencing just about every architectural style, and glittering with gilded ornamentation, polished marble and glass. Built in 1905, it was the culminating master-work of the Bruges architect Louis Delacenserie (1838–1909).

Palais de Justice, Brussels

9 Palais de Justice, Brussels

This colossal pile, which dominates the city skyline, still serves as a law court, so it's normally possible to enter during working hours on weekdays. It was the biggest building in Europe when completed in 1883 after 17 years of construction, and the interior is as vast and elaborate as the exterior. Renovations have been ongoing since 2003 (see p76).

10 Churches

Many of the churches are free to enter (although you are invited to leave a donation). There are exceptions, such as Antwerp Cathedral.

TOP 10 MONEY-SAVING TIPS

Centraal station Antwerp

1 Belgian railways offer numerous discounts, eg for weekend travel, the over 65s, children under 12. Visit www.belgianrail.be.

2 Hotel prices fluctuate a lot according to business travel patterns and tourist flow. You can find bargain rates at weekends in Brussels; weekdays off-season are cheaper in Bruges.

3 Check if breakfast is included in your hotel price. If not, breakfast in the hotel will add €10–25 per person per night to your stay.

4 Car parking is most expensive in city centres, and much cheaper – free, even – on the outskirts. Park and walk to Bruges, Antwerp or Ghent, or take the park and ride to Brussels.

5 A 24/48/72-hour pass or preloadable multi-journey MOBIB Basic card can save money on public transport. This is particularly relevant in Brussels, where you may wish to travel to the museums and sights of Outer Brussels, beyond normal walking distance.

6 Museum passes allow you to visit several museums in a given city for a single, reduced price.

7 In restaurants, fixed-price set-menus – particularly at lunchtime – can be real bargains.

8 Belgium is famous for its *frites* (chips), and a good chip stall (*friterie/frietkot*) can provide a cheap Belgian meal.

9 Picnics are a great way to save money. Delicatessens, bread shops and pâtisseries offer great prepared food – sandwiches, flans, tarts, tubs of salad.

10 Visitors from outside the EU can reclaim most sales tax (TVA/BWT) on purchases above a minimum value of €125 from any one shop. Visit www.brusselsairport.be.

🔟 **Festivals and Events**

Brass section of an orchestra performing at the Festival van Vlaanderen

① Festival van Vlaanderen
Dates are mainly Jun–Oct
■ www.festival.be

An impressive programme of classical music – as well as jazz, world music and dance – takes place across Flanders every summer and autumn, with performances in the main venues, as well as in churches and other historic buildings.

② Plantation du Meiboom, Brussels
9 Aug (1:30pm onwards)

This jolly slice of ancient folklore dates back to 1213. Led by the Confrérie des Compagnons de Saint-Laurent, dressed in wacky costumes, and accompanied by seven traditional giant figures, the participants parade a may tree around central Brussels, before planting it on the corner of Rue du Marais and Rue des Sables.

③ Foire du Midi, Brussels
Mid-Jul–mid-Aug

This big, rollicking, noisy late-summer fun fair set out along the Boulevard du Midi has the newest rides plus dodgems, roller coasters and all the other old favourites.

④ Heilig Bloedprocessie, Bruges
Ascension Day (May)

Bruges' biggest day out, the Procession of the Holy Blood follows an 800-year-old tradition: 40 days after Easter, the sacred relic of the Holy Blood is paraded around the streets in a colourful, spectacular, but at heart solemn procession featuring sumptuous medieval and biblical costumes.

⑤ Fête de Saint-Nicolas, throughout Belgium
6 Dec

The Feast of St Nicholas (Sinterklaas in Dutch) is celebrated by children with even greater enthusiasm than Christmas. St Nicholas (the original Santa Claus), dressed as the Bishop of Myra, walks the streets with his sidekick Zwarte Piet, and children receive presents, as well as sweets and *speculoos* biscuits.

⑥ Gentse Floraliën, Ghent
Late Apr (next in 2021)

Now taking place in four locations in the city centre (as opposed to just the Flanders Expo halls), this vast flower show is held once every five years.

Exhibit at Gentse Floraliën, Ghent

Ghent's flower-growing industry is famous above all for its begonias, azaleas, rhododendrons and roses.

⑦ Praalstoet van de Gouden Boom, Bruges
Late Aug (next in 2017)

First performed in 1958, the Pageant of the Golden Tree takes place in Bruges every five years or so. In a vast costumed parade, the people of the city evoke the glory days of the Burgundian era.

⑧ Ommegang, Brussels
First Tue & Thu in Jul

In Brussels' most spectacular parade, some 2,000 participants, dressed as Renaissance nobles, guildsmen, mounted soldiers and entertainers, perform an *ommegang* (tour) in the Grand Place. It's a tradition said to date back to 1549.

Ommegang parade, Brussels

⑨ Reiefeest, Bruges
Last 10 days of Aug (next in 2018)

This festival, held every five years, celebrates the River Reie's role in the city's history. A series of historical scenes is performed at night at various points beside the water, creating a magical effect and bringing the city's architecture to life.

⑩ Toussaint, throughout Belgium
1–2 Nov

All Saints' Day is followed by the Jour des Morts, the Day of the Dead – a time when Belgians honour their departed by tidying up the graveyards and laying flowers – mainly chrysanthemums.

TOP 10 SPECTATOR SPORTS AND VENUES

1 Ronde van Vlaanderen
First Sun in Apr
Classic of the cycling calendar.

2 Liège-Bastogne-Liège
Third Sun in Apr
Oldest cycling classic in the World Cup.

3 Zesdaagse van Vlaanderen-Gent
MAP P6 ▪ **Late Nov** ▪ **'t Kuipke, Citadelpark, Ghent**
One of the most important meetings for European speed cycling.

4 Memorial Van Damme
MAP F1 ▪ **Sep** ▪ **Stade Roi Baudouin, Brussels**
Important athletics meeting.

5 20 km of Brussels
Last Sun in May
Brussels' mini-marathon.

6 Belgian Grand Prix
Spa-Francorchamps ▪ **Late Aug**
A must for all committed petrol-heads.

7 Hippodrome Wellington, Ostend
Horseracing every Monday in July and August (harness and flatracing).

8 King Baudouin Stadium
MAP F1 ▪ **Ave du Marathon 135, 1020 BRU (Laeken)** ▪ **02 474 39 40**
Athletics, cycle meetings and international soccer matches.

9 Constant Vanden Stock Stadium
MAP F2 ▪ **Avenue Théo Verbeeck, 1070 BRU (Anderlecht)** ▪ **02 529 40 67 (for tickets)** ▪ **www.rsca.be**
The home ground of RSC Anderlecht.

10 Jan Breydel Stadium (Olympiapark)
Olympialaan 74, 8200 Bruges (Sint-Andries) ▪ **050 40 21 21** ▪ **www.clubbrugge.be**
Stadium shared by Club Brugge and Cercle Brugge.

Athletes at Memorial Van Damme

🔟 Excursions

The stunning town hall, Leuven

1 Leuven
Tourist Office: Naamsestraat 3
■ 016 20 30 20 ■ www.leuven.be

The old university town of Leuven (French: Louvain) has a deep charm, derived from its compact human scale and many historic buildings – chief among them the Stadhuis, the most beautiful Gothic town hall of them all with its lace-like detail.

2 Walibi Belgium
Belgium's biggest and best-known theme park – a good day out for the kids *(see p57)*.

3 Forêt de Soignes
Drève du Rouge-Cloître 4
■ www.foret-de-soignes.be

The magnificent ancient beech forests of Soignes provide a splendid landscape for walking or cycling – particularly in autumn, when the beech trees turn golden. There are two arboretums, at Groenendaal and Tervuren, and an information centre on the site of the 14th-century Abbaye du Rouge-Cloître.

4 Namur
Tourist Office: Place de la Station ■ 081 24 64 49
■ www.namurtourisme.be

An attractive town on the confluence of the Meuse and Sambre rivers, Namur is known for its mighty Citadelle perched dramatically on a steep-sided hill.

5 Mechelen
Tourist Office: Hallestraat 2–4
■ 070 22 00 08
■ www.toerismemechelen.be

Mechelen (French: Malines) was a proud trading city in the Burgundian era, and centre of power under Margaret of Austria (1507–15; 1519–30). Dominating the city is the vast bell-tower of Sint-Romboutskathedraal.

6 Lier
Tourist Office: Grote Markt 58
■ 038 00 05 55 ■ www.visitlier.be

This charming little town to the southeast of Antwerp has a handsome collection of historic buildings clustered around the Grote

Charming buildings line the water at Lier

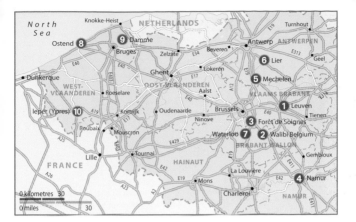

Markt, but its most famous possession is the Zimmertoren, a 14th-century watch-tower with its fascinating Centenary Clock.

Butte de Lion mound, Waterloo

7 Waterloo
Route du Lion 252–4, 1420 Braine-l'Alleud ∎ 023 85 19 12 ∎ Open 9:30am–6:30pm daily (Oct–Mar: 10am–6pm) ∎ Adm ∎ www.waterloo1815.be

Near Waterloo, 15 km (9 miles) south of Brussels, Napoleon was finally defeated. The battlefield has been a tourist site virtually since the battle itself. The new 1815 Memorial visitor centre is a good place to start.

8 Ostend
Tourist Office: Monacoplein 2 ∎ 059 70 11 99 ∎ www.visitoostende.be

Ostend (spelt Oostende locally) is famous as a resort and for its excellent seafood. It also has surprisingly good collections of art in the Mu.ZEE, featuring local artist James Ensor and the Symbolists.

9 Damme
Tourist Office: Huyse de Grote Sterre, Jacob van Maerlantstraat 3 ∎ 050 28 86 10 ∎ www.damme-online.com

A pretty cluster of late-medieval buildings is all that remains of the once-prosperous town at the head of the canal to Bruges. A pleasant excursion by boat, bus or bicycle.

10 Ieper (Ypres)
In Flanders Fields: Lakenhallen, Grote Markt 34 ∎ 057 23 92 20 ∎ Open Apr–mid-Nov: 10am–6pm daily; mid-Nov–Mar: 10am–5pm Tue–Sun. Closed 3 weeks in Jan ∎ Adm ∎ www.toerismeieper.be

Ieper (French: Ypres) was one of the great medieval trading cities of Flanders. Its historic past was all but erased when it became the focus of bitter trench warfare in World War I. Today it is a centre for visits to the trenches and the cemeteries, and site of the Menin Gate, the memorial arch marking the road along which soldiers marched. But the real draw is "In Flanders Fields", a museum depicting the background of the war, its experiences and horrors – a richly informative and moving experience.

Brussels, Bruges, Antwerp & Ghent Area by Area

Steenhouwersdijk, one of the most pictureque
stretches of the canal, Bruges

TOP 10 Central Brussels

Central Brussels is contained within a clearly defined shape called the Pentagon. Nowadays this outline is formed by a ring road called the Petite Ceinture, which follows the path of the old city walls. Little remains of the walls, but one old city gate, the Porte de Hal, still stands, and gives an indication of just how massive the fortifications were. Most of historic Brussels is within these bounds, including both the commercial and popular districts of the Lower Town, and the aristocratic quarter of the Upper Town, which includes the Royal Palace. As well as cultural gems, you will find places to stay and eat, good shops, and vibrant cafés and bars.

AREA MAP OF CENTRAL BRUSSELS

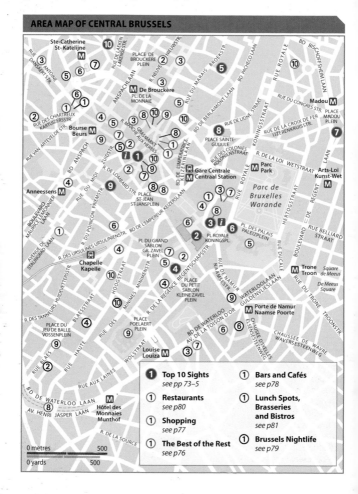

① **Top 10 Sights** *see pp 73–5*		① **Bars and Cafés** *see p78*	
① **Restaurants** *see p80*		① **Lunch Spots, Brasseries and Bistros** *see p81*	
① **Shopping** *see p77*			
① **The Best of the Rest** *see p76*		① **Brussels Nightlife** *see p79*	

The impressive Grand Place during the Tapis des Fleurs flower festival

1 The Grand Place

No trip to Brussels would be complete without a visit to the Grand Place – even if it's just to stock up on some Belgian biscuits or chocolates. A remarkable legacy of the city's Gothic and Renaissance past, it is also a monument to the values and ingenuity of the artisans and merchants who were the architects of Brussels' prosperity (see pp14–15).

The Card Players by De Braekeleer, Musées Royaux des Beaux-Arts

2 Musées Royaux des Beaux-Arts

The premier art gallery of Belgium focuses almost exclusively on Flemish and Belgian art, and is more rewarding for it. Highlights include rare works by Pieter Bruegel the Elder and the exhilarating Rubens collection. It is interlinked with the Fin-de-Siècle Museum and the Magritte Museum (see pp18–19).

3 Musée des Instruments de Musique

The famous "mim" collection of historical and contemporary musical instruments is housed in the remarkable Art Nouveau department store known as "Old England". A visitor guidance system brings the exhibits to life (see pp20–21)

4 Sablon

MAP C4 ■ Rue de la Régence 3B ■ Church: Open 8am–6pm Mon–Fri, 9:30am–6pm Sat, 10am–6pm Sun

The name Sablon refers to the sandy marshland that occupied this site until it was reclaimed in the 17th century. The Place du Grand Sablon is a centre for antiques and is home to leading chocolate makers: Pierre Marcolini and Wittamer. The Place du Petit Sablon park is adorned with 48 statues of the medieval guilds of Brussels. Separating the two is the Église Notre-Dame du Sablon.

Église Notre-Dame du Sablon

A visitor browses comic designs at the Comics Art Museum

5 Comics Art Museum

Reflecting the huge popularity of comic-strip books in Belgium – and, indeed, most of continental Europe – this unique museum, formerly known as the Centre Belge de la Bande Dessinée, is a shrine to the art form. Archive material and other exhibits focus above all on Belgian contributors to the genre – most notably, of course, on Hergé, the creator of Tintin (see pp26–7).

Underground at Palais Coudenberg

6 Palais Coudenberg

MAP D4 ■ Place des Palais 7
■ 02 500 45 54 ■ Open 9:30am–5pm
Tue–Fri, 10am–6pm Sat & Sun;
10am–6pm daily Jul & Aug ■ Adm

Accessed via the BELvue Museum (see p76), this archaeological site was once the medieval Coudenberg Palace that stood on Place Royale. The palace was the seat of residence for the Duchy of Brabant and then the Governors of the Netherlands for more than 600 years until it burned down in 1731. The highlight is the impressive Aula Magna banqueting hall, which was the scene of King Charles V's abdication in 1555.

7 Musée Charlier

MAP E3 ■ Avenue des Arts 16
■ 02 220 26 91 ■ Open noon–5pm
Mon–Thu, 10am–1pm Fri ■ Adm
■ www.charliermuseum.be

Brussels is a city of grand old 19th-century mansions, or *maisons de maître*. This museum provides a rare opportunity to see inside one. The original owner, Henri van Curtsem, commissioned Victor Horta (see p23) to redesign the interior. In the hands of van Curtsem's adoptive heir, sculptor Guillaume Charlier, the mansion became a centre for Brussels' avant-garde. On his death in 1925, Charlier left the house to the city, and it retains much of the decor of his era. There are works displayed by leading artists of the time, such as James Ensor, Léon Frédéric, Fernand Khnopff and Rik Wouters, plus an impressive collection of antique furniture.

8 Cathédrale des Saints Michel et Gudule

MAP D3 ■ Parvis Sainte-Gudule
■ 02 217 83 45 ■ Open 7am–6pm
Mon–Fri, 8:30am–3:30pm Sat, 2–6pm
Sun ■ Adm only for Museum of
Church Treasures and Crypt

Brussels' largest and finest church was built from 1226 onwards and showcases over 300 years' worth of architectural design. Highlights inside include an enormous Baroque oak pulpit, splendid Renaissance stained-glass windows, and access to the treasury and preserved remnants of the old Romanesque

A DAY IN THE CENTRE

church that once stood here. Dedicated to St Michael, patron saint of the city, the cathedral also acknowledges in its name St Gudule, a local 8th-century saint who outfoxed the Devil. The cathedral is often used for royal weddings and state funerals.

⑨ Manneken-Pis

In Brussels you can't avoid this cheeky chap, famously relieving himself with carefree abandon, just as little boys do. Among other things, he's on postcards, T-shirts, key rings and corkscrews. So why not take a pilgrimage to see the real thing – a tiny bronze statue – and bask in the happy absurdity of it all? It must be worth a photograph *(see p16)*.

⑩ Église St-Jean-Baptiste au Béguinage

MAP B1 ■ Place du Béguinage
■ 02 217 87 42 ■ Open 10am–5pm Tue–Sat, 10am–8pm Sun

Considered to be one of the country's prettiest churches, this Baroque beauty belonged to a *béguinage (see p92)* and dates from the 17th century. Parts of the church are occupied by a group of refugees.

Église St-Jean-Baptiste

▶ MORNING

Start off with the essentials: a stroll around the **Grand Place** *(see pp14–15)* and a trip to the **Manneken-Pis** *(see p16)*, stopping for a waffle at the **Dandoy** shop at Rue Charles Buls 14 on the way. Now head back to the **Bourse** *(see p16)*, and go west along Rue Dansaert, the street for cutting-edge fashion. Turn right at the Rue du Vieux Marché aux Grains and walk up to the **Église Sainte-Catherine**, a church designed in 1854 by Joseph Poelaert, also responsible for the Palais de Justice. It stands on reclaimed land at the head of a canal now covered over by the Place Sainte-Catherine. This was the site of the old fish market, and is still famous for its fish restaurants – an ideal place to stop for lunch.

AFTERNOON

Walk back east, stopping at the **Cathédrale des Saints Michel et Gudule** before heading up the hill to Rue Royale. Take a stroll in the pleasant **Parc de Bruxelles**, then walk south to the **Palais Royal** *(see p76)* and the elegant 17th-century Place Royale, with its statue of the 11th-century crusader Godefroy de Bouillon. You're now a stone's throw from both the **Musées Royaux des Beaux-Arts** *(see pp18–19)* and the **Musée des Instruments de Musique** *(see pp20–21)*. After this, you'll probably need refreshments, so continue down the Rue de la Régence to the cafés and chocolate shops of **Sablon** *(see p73)*.

See map on p72 ←

The Best of the Rest

1 Galeries Royales Saint-Hubert

When it opened in 1847, this very elegant shopping arcade was the first and grandest in Europe *(see p16)*.

2 Musée du Costume et de la Dentelle

On display are exquisite examples of costume and lace, an industry that employed 10,000 women in mid-19th-century Brussels *(see p16)*.

3 Place des Martyrs

MAP C2

The 445 "martyrs" killed in the Belgian Revolution of 1830 were laid to rest in a crypt beneath this square.

4 Église Notre-Dame de la Chapelle

MAP B4 ▪ Place de la Chapelle ▪ Open Nov–Feb: 9am–6pm daily, Mar–Oct: 9am–7pm daily

This large, atmospheric church is like something out of a Bruegel painting – aptly so, since Pieter Bruegel the Elder is buried here.

5 Palais Royal and BELvue Museum

MAP D4 ▪ Place des Palais. Palais Royal: 02 551 20 20; Open Jul–mid-Sep: 10:30am–4:30pm Tue–Sun ▪ BELvue Museum: 02 500 45 54; Open 9:30am–5pm Tue–Fri; Jul & Aug, weekends: 10am–6pm ▪ Adm

See how the other half lived in the grand rooms of the Royal Palace. A former hotel next to the palace houses a museum devoted to the history of Belgium since 1830.

6 Palais de Charles de Lorraine

MAP C4 ▪ Place du Musée 1 ▪ Open 9am–5pm first Sat of every month (closed Jul & Aug) ▪ Adm

This suite of 18th-century rooms contains a small but interesting exhibition of furniture, porcelain, clocks and other artifacts.

7 Cinematek

MAP D4 ▪ Rue Baron Horta 9 ▪ 02 551 19 19 ▪ Open daily ▪ Adm ▪ www.cinematek.be

A bijou cinema with a fascinating collection tracing the early history of the moving image in the foyer.

8 Porte de Hal

MAP B6 ▪ Boulevard du Midi 150 ▪ 02 534 34 50 ▪ Open 9:30am–5pm Tue–Fri, 10am–5pm Sat & Sun ▪ Adm (free from 1pm first Wed of month)

The sole surviving gate of the 14th-century city walls houses a museum of defences and history.

9 Palais de Justice

MAP B5 ▪ Place Poelaert ▪ Open 9am–3pm Mon–Fri

There is something gloriously megalomaniac about this vast Neo-Classical pile.

10 Musée du Jouet

MAP E2 ▪ Rue de l'Association 24 ▪ 02 219 61 68 ▪ Open 10am–noon & 2–6pm daily ▪ Adm

This delightful toy museum will appeal to both children and adults.

Entrance of the Palais de Justice

Shopping

1 Galeries Royales Saint-Hubert

Home to luxury shops including jewellers and crystal makers (see p16).

2 Rue Neuve
MAP C2

This pedestrianized shopping street close to the city centre features many of the main European fashion chains and a large Inno department store at the northern end.

3 Rue Antoine Dansaert
MAP A2

Ignore the shoddy environs: this is the place for cutting-edge fashion. All the Antwerp designers are represented in the shops here, and there are several outlets for notable Belgian fashion labels.

Christmas market stall

4 Christmas Market
MAP B3

From early December to early January, this market offers all things Christmassy – crafts, decorations, gifts – in the streets around the Bourse and on Quai aux Briques.

5 Place du Grand Sablon
MAP C4

There are antiques shops fronting the square, but poke around in some of the side passages as well. Two of the finest chocolatiers, Wittamer and Pierre Marcolini, are here (see p63).

6 Avenue Louise and Galerie de la Toison d'Or
MAP C6/D5

Top-name international couturiers, including Chanel and Hermès, can

Second-hand books, Galerie Bortier

be found along Avenue Louise and the adjoining Boulevard de Waterloo. The covered Galerie de la Toison d'Or, a little further to the east, is also a major shopping hub.

7 Around the Grand Place
MAP B3/C3

Rue Marché aux Herbes, Rue Marché au Charbon and Rue du Midi are good for independent boutiques, jewellers, bookshops and food shops.

8 Galerie Bortier
MAP C3

Smaller than the Galeries Royales Saint-Hubert, but just as elegant. Here you'll find second-hand books, prints, postcards and posters.

9 Rue Blaes and Place du Jeu de Balle
MAP B5

Place du Jeu de Balle has a daily flea market (6am–2pm) selling antiques, junk and curios, and there are similar shops along Rue Blaes.

10 Galerie Agora
MAP C3

This maze-like covered arcade sells inexpensive T-shirts, leather goods, costume jewellery and incense.

See map on p72 ←

Bars and Cafés

1 Le Greenwich
MAP B2 ▪ Rue des Chartreux 7

An established Brussels favourite, especially popular with an avid chess-playing crowd. It was a former hang-out of Magritte.

A game of chess at Le Greenwich

2 Le Roy d'Espagne
MAP C3 ▪ Grand Place 1

A famous watering-hole in the old bakers' guildhouse. There is a medieval air to the interior decor. Also serves light meals.

3 Au Bon Vieux Temps
MAP C3 ▪ Impasse St-Nicolas 4

Blink and you'll miss this traditional 17th-century tavern tucked down a side street off Rue du Marché aux Herbes. This is a great spot for escaping the bustle outside.

4 Moeder Lambic
MAP B3 ▪ Place Fontainas 8

The central Brussels branch of the revered Saint-Gilles "beer academy", this splendid bar offers hundreds of mainly Belgian beers, dozens of them on tap, and all are listed in the catalogue. If you can't decide which, ask the staff: they are experts and always happy to help.

5 Le Cirio
MAP B3 ▪ Rue de la Bourse 18

Another classic, Le Cirio has been open since 1886 and is famous for its *half-en-half* – a mix of still and sparkling white wine.

6 La Fleur en Papier Dore
MAP B4
▪ Rue des Alexiens 53–55

A rare survivor among the traditional sort of Belgian pub-cum-café known as *estaminets*. Pictures and mementos recall its connections with the Surrealist movement. Good Belgian beers and pub food.

7 Wittamer
MAP C4
▪ Place du Grand Sablon 12–13

The world-class chocolatier has a seating area where you can sample its heavenly products with a cup of tea or coffee on the side.

8 mim
MAP D4
▪ Rue Montagne de la Cour 2

The Musée des Instruments de Musique's spectacular café *(see pp20–21)*.

9 Bonnefooi
MAP B3
▪ Steenstraat/Rue des Pierres 8

This lively bar draws a young crowd with its live music on week nights and DJs at the weekend. Great atmosphere especially in summer.

10 À La Mort Subite
MAP C2 ▪ Rue Montagne aux Herbes Potagères 7

"Sudden Death" may sound rather alarming, but this famous bar, redesigned in Rococo style in 1926, is named after a card game.

À La Mort Subite

Brussels Nightlife

Archiduc in full swing

1 Archiduc
MAP B2 ■ Rue Antoine Dansaert 6–8 ■ 02 512 06 52

This legendary 1930s Art Deco bar – designed like a cruise liner – has entertained all the jazz greats. The place picks up after midnight.

2 Fuse
MAP B5 ■ Rue Blaes 208 ■ 02 511 97 89

Behind the gritty industrial exterior lies the best club in town. World-class DJs spin a mix of techno and drum 'n' bass.

3 Club Avenue
MAP C6 ■ Avenue de la Toison d'Or 44 ■ www.clubavenue.be

A glitzy Upper Town nightclub where international funk blends perfectly with cutting-edge French rap and R&B artists.

4 Le Bazaar
MAP B5 ■ Rue des Capucins 63 ■ 02 511 26 00

It's hard to miss this club, which is over two floors and hosts world music and parties most Friday and Saturday nights. International DJs also play here. Living up to its name, the decoration is rather "bazaar".

5 The Music Village
MAP B3 ■ Rue des Pierres 50 ■ 02 513 13 45

Jazz and blues bar with live concerts taking place every night: 8:30pm on weeknights; 9pm on weekends. Dinner is available either before or during the performances.

6 Spirito Martini
MAP C6 ■ Rue Stassart 18 ■ 483 580 697

Housed in a former Anglican church, this swish nightclub/restaurant features a sumptuous gold and crystal decor, beautiful lighting and a vast dancefloor.

7 Madame Moustache
MAP B2 ■ 5 -7 Quai au Bois à Brûler ■ 0489 739 912

A retro club (1950s–80s) and concert venue, featuring rock'n'roll, swing, funk and jazz. It prides itself on its quirky, cabaret atmosphere.

8 Le You
MAP C3 ■ Rue Duquesnoy 18 ■ 02 639 14 00

This popular club enjoys a lively central location. The music ranges from electro and house to 1980s retro and R&B. On Sundays, it attracts a predominantly gay crowd.

9 The Flat
MAP D5 ■ Rue de la Reinette 12

At this town house lounge bar you can sip your cocktail in the lounge, bedroom or bathroom!

10 Havana
MAP B5 ■ Rue de l'Épée 4 ■ 02 502 12 24

The ambience may be Latin but the music comes in all varieties at this lively dance club. Open late Thursday and all night at weekends. There are four bars and a restaurant.

See map on p72 ←

Restaurants

① Comme Chez Soi
MAP B4 ■ Place Rouppe 23
■ 02 512 29 21 ■ Closed Sun, Mon,
Tue L, Wed L ■ €€€

Brussels' most celebrated restaurant
is family-run and has two Michelin
stars. For a taste of the superlative,
innovative French cuisine, be sure
to book weeks ahead.

L'Ecailler du Palais Royal

② L'Ecailler du Palais Royal
MAP C4 ■ Rue Bodenbroek 18 ■ 02
512 87 51 ■ Closed Sun, Aug ■ €€€

One of Brussels' most prestigious
fish restaurants, this quiet, refined
establishment attracts a mature
clientele with its classic cuisine.

③ Belga Queen
MAP C2 ■ Rue du Fossé-aux-
Loups 32 ■ 02 217 21 87 ■ €€€

This stylish restaurant is housed in
an ornate former bank. The menu,
with a French–Belgium influence
offers better value at lunchtime.

④ Kwint
MAP C4 ■ Mont des Arts 1
■ 02 505 95 95 ■ Closed Sun ■ €€€

Customers dine on first-class
fish and pasta, beneath a world-
renowned Arne Quinze sculpture,
at this elegant restaurant.

⑤ Sea Grill, SAS Radisson
MAP C2 ■ Rue du Fossé-aux-
Loups 47 ■ 02 218 08 00 ■ Closed Sat,
Sun ■ €€€

Boasting two Michelin stars, this fish
restaurant offers refined dining.

⑥ La Belle Maraîchère
MAP B2 ■ Place Sainte-
Catherine 11a ■ 02 512 97 59
■ Closed Wed, Thu ■ €€€

A favourite with locals for decades,
this timeless wood-panelled
restaurant serves top-rate
fish dishes.

⑦ Cospaia
MAP C5 ■ Rue Crespel 1
■ 02 513 03 03 ■ Closed Mon, Tue,
Sat L, Sun ■ €€

This sleek, sexy restaurant, located
on the southern edge of the Pentagon,
serves fusion cuisine. During the day,
opt for the white dining room; at night,
the black room is more romantic.

⑧ Aux Armes de Bruxelles
MAP C3 ■ Rue des Bouchers 13
■ 02 511 55 50 ■ €€

Founded in 1921, Aux Armes de
Bruxelles is an institution, praised
for its white-linen elegance and
impeccable Belgian cooking.

⑨ Restaurant Vincent
MAP C3 ■ Rue des Dominicains
8–10 ■ 02 511 26 07 ■ €€

Dine on mussels and flambéed
steaks in a room decorated with
old marine murals.

⑩ L'Idiot du Village
MAP B4 ■ Rue Notre-Seigneur
19 ■ 02 502 55 82 ■ Closed Sat, Sun
■ €€€

A long-standing favourite with locals
who consistently praise the inventive
menus and shabby-chic style.

L'Idiot du Village

Lunch Spots, Brasseries and Bistros

PRICE CATEGORIES

For a three-course meal for one with half a bottle of wine (or equivalent meal), taxes and extra charges.

€ under €40   €€ €40- 60   €€€ over €60

1 Cap d'Argent
MAP D3 ▪ Rue Ravenstein 10 ▪ 02 513 09 19 ▪ Closed Sun ▪ €

A no-frills bistro admired for tasty Belgian classics and great service.

2 In 't Spinnekopke
MAP A3 ▪ Place du Jardin-aux-Fleurs 1 ▪ 02 511 86 95 ▪ Closed Sun L ▪ €

An appealing *estaminet* (traditional pub) that stands by its 18th-century heritage to present a menu of fine Belgian-Bruxellois dishes.

3 Bozar Brasserie
MAP D3 ▪ Rue Baron Horta 3 ▪ 02 503 00 00 ▪ Closed Sun, Mon ▪ €€€

Designed by Victor Horta in 1928, this Art Deco gem is in beautiful condition after a loving renovation. The lauded chef prepares faultless Belgian cuisine.

4 Les Petits Oignons
MAP C5 ▪ Rue de la Régence 25 ▪ 02 511 76 15 ▪ €€

It's a treat to eat at this elegant brasserie, which receives glowing reviews. The carefully selected wine list also contributes to its popularity.

5 Le Crachin
MAP B2 ▪ Rue de Flandre 12 ▪ 02 502 13 00 ▪ €

A jovial café serving sweet and savoury traditional Breton pancakes with mugs of Brittany cider.

6 Le Pain Quotidien
MAP B2 ▪ Rue Antoine Dansaert 16a ▪ 02 502 23 61 ▪ €

Selling excellent bread with delicious fillings, as well as tempting pastries, Le Pain Quotidien ("Daily Bread") is a huge success. This is the most central of the many city branches.

7 Chez Patrick
MAP C3 ▪ Rue des Chapeliers 6 ▪ 02 511 98 15 ▪ Closed Sun, Mon ▪ €€

This cherished and popular restaurant refuses to change or diverge from its traditions of solid, good-value, truly Belgian cooking. The prices are reasonable considering its location near Grand Place.

Art Deco style Taverne du Passage

8 Taverne du Passage
MAP C3 ▪ Galerie de la Reine 30 ▪ 02 512 37 31 ▪ €€

A traditional 1930s Belgian diner with accomplished waiters and an enthusiastic local clientele. The fish dishes are excellent.

9 't Kelderke
MAP C3 ▪ Grand Place 15 ▪ 02 513 73 44 ▪ €

A 17th-century cellar-restaurant delivering feasts of Belgian cuisine. The good food attracts appreciative locals as well as tourists.

10 Chez Léon
MAP C3 ▪ Rue des Bouchers 18 ▪ 02 511 14 15 ▪ €

Established in 1893, this restaurant is a *moules-frites* specialist that has become an international brand.

See map on p72

TOP 10 Outer Brussels

Parc du Cinquantenaire

Over the centuries, Brussels expanded beyond the old city walls, gradually absorbing neighbouring towns and villages. These outlying communes – such as Ixelles, Saint-Gilles and Anderlecht – still retain their distinctive characters. As a result, there is huge variety across outer Brussels. An excellent public transport system makes it easy to get around these suburbs, and the highlights listed here are worth the journey.

1 The Atomium
MAP F1 (inset) ▪ Square de l'Atomium, 1020 BRU (Laeken) ▪ 02 475 47 75 ▪ Open 10am–6pm daily ▪ Adm ▪ www.atomium.be

This giant model of an iron crystal was built as Belgium's exhibit at Brussels' 1958 Universal Exposition. It stands 102 m (335 ft) tall and has nine 18 m (59 ft) diameter spheres.

2 Horta Museum
A symphony in Art Nouveau design (see pp22–3).

AREA MAP OF OUTER BRUSSELS

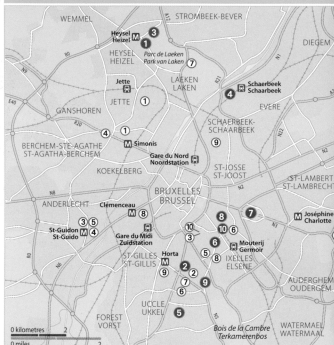

The Atomium

3 Art and Design Atomium Museum

MAP F1 ■ Place de Belgique, 1020 BRU (Laeken) ■ 02 669 49 29 ■ Open 10am–6pm Wed–Mon ■ Adm ■ www.adamuseum.be

In the shadow of the Atomium, this museum focuses solely on modern design. The main highlight is the huge Plasticarium collection of the largest plastic design objects in Europe, from playful Pop Art to the iconic Post-Modern cantilever chair.

4 Train World

MAP G2 ■ Place Princesse Élisabeth 5, 1030 BRU (Schaerbeek) ■ 02 224 74 98 ■ Open 10am–5pm Tue–Sun (last entry 3:30pm) ■ Adm ■ www.trainworld.be

This long-awaited railway museum opened in 2015, gathering together the impressive historic collection of Belgian national railways (NMBS/SNCB) for the first time. It contains locomotives dating back to the 1840s, plus carriages and all sorts of railway paraphernalia, theatrically presented with dramatic lighting, sound effects and imaginative props that help to personalize the exhibits. The beautiful and immaculately restored 19th-century Schaerbeek station is the main hub (accessible by train, tram and bus), with adjacent modern, purpose-built exhibition halls housing the main exhibits.

Van Buuren Museum

5 Van Buuren Museum

MAP G3 ■ Ave Léo Errera 41, 1180 BRU (Uccle) ■ 02 343 48 51 ■ Museum & garden open 2–5:30pm daily ■ Adm ■ www.museumvanbuuren.com

This beautifully preserved Art Deco home of David and Alice van Buuren has excellent furniture and stained glass, plus contemporary paintings.

6 Musée d'Ixelles

MAP E7 ▪ Rue J Van Volsem 71, 1050 BRU (Ixelles) ▪ 02 515 64 21 ▪ Open 9:30am–5pm Tue–Sun; closed Mon and public hols ▪ Adm ▪ www.museumofixelles.irisnet.be

It's well worth the trek to this southern suburb for this small but excellent municipal art collection. It has a number of minor works by great masters, including Rembrandt, Delacroix and Picasso, as well as an excellent collection of posters by Toulouse-Lautrec. This is also a good place to see more work by Symbolists such as Léon Spilliaert and Léon Frédéric, the much-cherished sculpture and Fauve-style painting of Rik Wouters, as well as Surrealist paintings, some by Magritte.

Art displayed at the Musée d'Ixelles

7 Parc du Cinquantenaire

MAP H4 ▪ Parc du Cinquantenaire, 1000 BRU ▪ Musées Royaux d'Art et d'Histoire: 02 741 72 11; open 9:30am–5pm Tue–Fri, 10am–5pm Sat–Sun; closed Mon and public hols; adm (free 1–5pm 1st Wed of month); www.kmkg-mrah.be ▪ Musée Royal de l'Armée: 02 737 78 11; open 9am–noon, 1–4:45pm; closed Mon and public hols; adm; www.klm-mra.be ▪ Autoworld: 02 736 41 65; open Apr–Sep: 10am–6pm daily, Oct–Mar: 10am–5pm daily; adm; www.autoworld.be

In 1880 King Léopold II staged a grand international fair to celebrate the 50th anniversary of the founding of his nation. The vast exhibition halls he erected, together with their successors, now contain a cluster of major museums. The most spectacular is the Musées Royaux d'Art et d'Histoire, a collection of treasures from around the

KING LÉOPOLD II

Belgium's second king reigned from 1865 to 1909, a time of great change in Europe. Léopold II was an enthusiast of modernization, and undertook many grand building projects. Determined to make Belgium a colonial power, he created and ruled the Belgian Congo. However, his regime there was brutal, and millions died under his reign.

world. Close by are the Musée Royal de l'Armée et d'Histoire Militaire (military museum) and Autoworld (collection of vintage cars). The park also contains the Atelier de Moulage, and the Pavillon Horta-Lambeaux, a Neo-Classical work by a young Victor Horta to house an erotic sculpture by Jef Lambeaux (1852–1908).

8 Parlement Européen and the Parlamentarium

MAP F5 ▪ Rue Wiertz 60, 1047 BRU ▪ 02 283 22 22 ▪ Audio tour open 10am & 3pm Mon–Thu, 10am Fri ▪ Parlamentarium open 1–6pm Mon, 9am–6pm Tue–Fri, 10am–6pm Sat & Sun ▪ www.europarl.europa.eu

EU politics may seem a dry, complex issue, but a trip to the European Parliament and its visitor centre will convince you otherwise. Free audio-guided tours of the Parliament are available, while the Parlamentarium explains the past, present and future of the EU in more detail. Visitors are provided with a multimedia handset,

Parlement européen

which guides them around the interactive displays. Meet the MEPs who shape European laws, listen to the multitude of EU languages in the Tunnel of Voices, and find out why the Parliament decamps from Brussels to Strasbourg every month.

9 Meunier Museum
MAP G2 ■ Rue de l'Abbaye 59, 1050 BRU (Ixelles) ■ 02 648 44 49 ■ Open 10am–noon, 12:45–5pm Tue–Fri; closed Mon, weekends and public hols ■ www.fine-arts-museum.be

Constantin Meunier (1831–1905) was one of the great sculptors of the late 19th century, famous for his distinctive bronzes of working people – especially *puddleurs* (forge workers). The museum occupies his former home, and contains some excellent examples of his work.

The Premature Burial, Antoine Wiertz

10 Wiertz Museum
MAP F5 ■ Rue Vautier 62, 1050 BRU (Ixelles) ■ 02 648 17 18 ■ Open 10am–noon, 12:45–5pm Tue–Fri; closed Mon, public hols and Sat–Sun (except for pre-booked groups) ■ www.fine-arts-museum.be

This is one of the most extraordinary museums in Brussels. Antoine Wiertz (1806–65) was an artist whose self-esteem far outstripped his talent. As a young man, he was egged on by patrons, and success went to his head. This grand studio was built so that he could paint works on a scale to rival Michelangelo. The grandiose canvases are interesting in themselves, but so too are the smaller works, many so macabre and moralistic they inspire both wonderment and mirth.

A WALK THROUGH THE BRUSSELS OF LÉOPOLD II

▶ MORNING

Put on your best walking shoes, because you're going to cover at least 5 km (3 miles) of pavement and take in half a dozen museums. You don't have to do them all, of course, and don't try this on a Monday, when most of the museums are closed. Start at the Schuman métro station in the heart of the European Quarter, close to the Justus Lipsius Building. If you're feeling fit, stride up Rue Archimède to admire the weirdest Art Nouveau building of them all – the **Hôtel Saint-Cyr** in Square Ambiorix (*see p48*). Otherwise, head into the **Parc du Cinquantenaire** (*see p84*) and take your pick of the museums. To refresh yourself, go to **Place Jourdan**, where there are numerous cafés and restaurants to suit all pockets.

AFTERNOON

Cross the Parc Léopold to visit the **Wiertz Museum**, then walk about 1 km (1000 yd) to the delightful **Musée d'Ixelles** (*see p84*). If you've had enough already, you could slink into the trendy **Café Belga** in the 1930s Flagey radio building (*see p87*); otherwise, push on down the Chaussée de Vleurgat to the **Meunier Museum**. Now you're only 10 minutes away from the **Horta Museum** (*see pp22–3*). From here you can get a tram home, or wander around the Art Nouveau houses in the vicinity (*see pp48–9*) and finish the day at **Le Clan des Belges** (*see p87*).

See map on pp82–3 ⟶

The Best of the Rest

1 Musée René Magritte
MAP F1 ▪ Rue Esseghem 135, 1090 BRU ▪ 02 428 26 26 ▪ Open 10am–6pm Wed–Sun ▪ Adm ▪ www.magrittemuseum.be
Magritte's modest former abode.

2 Musée du Tram
MAP G2 ▪ Ave de Tervuren 364B, 1150 BRU (Woluwe-Saint-Pierre) ▪ 02 515 31 08 ▪ Open Apr–Sep: 2–6pm Wed, 1–7pm Sat , Sun & public hols ▪ Adm ▪ www.trammuseumbrussels.be
A splendid collection of Brussels' historic trams, with tram rides.

3 Béguinage d'Anderlecht
MAP F2 ▪ Rue du Chapelain 8, 1070 BRU ▪ 02 521 13 83 ▪ Open 10am–noon, 2–5pm Tue–Sun ▪ Adm
Tiny *béguinage* (see p92), now a museum showing how the *béguines* 'ved.

Serres Royales de Laeken

4 Serres Royales de Laeken
MAP G1 ▪ Ave du Parc Royal (Domaine Royal), 1020 BRU ▪ 02 551 20 20 ▪ Open Apr–May ▪ Adm
Fabulous royal greenhouses.

5 Maison d'Érasme
MAP F2 ▪ Rue du Chapitre 31, 1070 BRU (Anderlecht) ▪ 02 521 13 83 ▪ Open 10am–6pm Tue–Sun ▪ Adm ▪ www.erasmushouse.museum
This charming red-brick house where Dutch humanist Erasmus stayed in 1521 is now a museum dedicated to his life.

Muséum des Sciences Naturelles

6 Muséum des Sciences Naturelles
MAP F5 ▪ Rue Vautier 29, 1000 BRU ▪ Open 9:30am–5pm Tue–Fri, 10am–6pm Sat, Sun & school hols ▪ Adm ▪ www.naturalsciences.be
See complete dinosaur skeletons.

7 Basilique Nationale du Sacré-Coeur
MAP F1 ▪ Parvis de la Basilique 1, 1081 BRU (Ganshoren) ▪ 02 421 16 60 ▪ Open Easter–Oct: 9am–5pm; Nov–Easter: 10am–4pm ▪ Adm for panorama only
The largest Art Deco building ever built? Remarkable view from its copper-green dome.

8 Cantillon
MAP A4 ▪ Rue Gheude 56, 1070 BRU (Anderlecht) ▪ 02 521 49 28 ▪ Open 10am–5pm Mon–Sat (last entry 4pm) ▪ Closed Wed, Sun & public hols ▪ Adm ▪ www.cantillon.be
A splendid dusty, old brewery.

9 Maison Autrique
MAP G2 ▪ Chaussée de Haecht 266, 1030 BRU (Schaerbeek) ▪ Open noon–6pm Wed–Sun ▪ Adm ▪ www.autrique.be
Victor Horta's first project (see p54).

10 Koninklijk Museum voor Midden-Afrika
MAP H2 ▪ Leuvensesteenweg 13, 3080 Tervuren ▪ 02 769 52 11 ▪ www.africamuseum.be
First-class Africa museum. Closed for renovation until 2017.

See map on pp82–3

Restaurants, Cafés and Bars

PRICE CATEGORIES

For a three-course meal for one with half a bottle of wine (or equivalent meal), taxes and extra charges.

€ under €40 €€ €40–60 €€€ over €60

1 Bruneau

MAP F1 ■ Ave Broustin 73–5, 1083 BRU (Ganshoren) ■ 02 421 70 70 ■ Closed Tue, Wed ■ €€€

This is one of Brussels' finest restaurants. Chef Jean-Pierre Bruneau has been given many esteemed awards for his exquisite seasonal French cuisine.

2 La Quincaillerie

MAP G2 ■ Rue du Page 45, 1050 BRU (Ixelles) ■ 02 533 98 33 ■ Closed Sun L ■ €€

The spectacular historic interior of this converted hardware store and the exciting menu more than make up for the gruff service.

3 Le Clan des Belges

MAP D6 ■ Rue de la Paix 20, 1050 BRU (Ixelles) ■ 02 511 11 21 ■ €

This lively brasserie is very popular with locals for its classic Belgian dishes at reasonable prices.

4 Le Chapeau Blanc

MAP F2 ■ Rue Wayez 200,1070 BRU (Anderlecht) ■ 02 520 02 02 ■ €€

"The White Hat" is a charming brasserie serving excellent mussels and oysters (in season), and steaks.

5 Rouge Tomate

MAP C6 ■ Ave Louise 190, 1050 BRU (Ixelles) ■ 02 647 70 44 ■ Closed Sat L & Sun ■ €€€

Dine out on Mediterranean fare, a perfect choice for vegetarians.

6 Le Balmoral Milk Bar

MAP G2 ■ Place Georges Brugmann 21, 1050 BRU (Ixelles) ■ 02 347 08 82 ■ Closed Mon & Tue ■ €

This popular "Happy Days"-style 1960s diner is praised for its burgers and milkshakes.

7 La Canne en Ville

MAP G2 ■ Rue de la Réforme 22, 1050 BRU (Ixelles) ■ 02 347 29 26 ■ Closed Sat L, Sun & weekends Jul & Aug ■ €€€

A delightful restaurant in a converted butcher's shop. The cooking is French-based.

8 Café Belga (Flagey building)

MAP G2 ■ Place Eugène Flagey, 1050 BRU (Ixelles) ■ 02 640 35 08 ■ www.cafebelga.be

Trendy café, set in an extraordinary 1930s Art Deco Flagey radio building, that draws a young arty crowd. Also a thriving music venue.

9 Moeder Lambic

MAP G2 ■ Rue de Savoie 68, 1060 BRU (Saint-Gilles) ■ 02 544 16 99

A welcoming pub devoted to beer, with 450 kinds on offer.

10 L'Ultime Atome

MAP D5 ■ Rue St Boniface 14, 1050 BRU (Ixelles) ■ 02 513 48 84 ■ Open daily ■ €

Trendy brasserie where locals come to drink artisan beers and French red wine.

L'Ultime Atome

🔟 Bruges

In the Middle Ages, Bruges was one of Europe's most prosperous cities. Its wealth derived from trade that brought silks, furs, Asian carpets, wine, fruits, and even exotic pets to its busy network of canals. In about 1500 Bruges fell from grace and slumbered for four centuries. It remained a pocket-sized medieval city, its poverty alleviated by almshouses, pious institutions, and a cottage industry supplying lace. In the late 19th century, antiquarians recognized Bruges as a historic gem, and began a campaign of preservation. In addition to many hotels, restaurants and bars, Bruges has famous art collections, and is a walkable city with surprises on every corner.

AREA MAP OF BRUGES

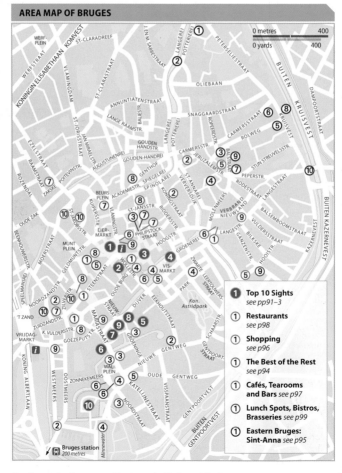

1	**Top 10 Sights** see pp91–3
①	**Restaurants** see p98
①	**Shopping** see p96
①	**The Best of the Rest** see p94
①	**Cafés, Tearooms and Bars** see p97
①	**Lunch Spots, Bistros, Brasseries** see p99
①	**Eastern Bruges: Sint-Anna** see p95

Previous pages Restaurants illuminate the Markt at night, Bruges

Attractive gabled buildings lining the Markt

1 The Markt
MAP K4

The central marketplace of Bruges still retains much of its original outline, flanked by old step-gabled guildhouses, but the Provinciaal Hof (former local government) building on the eastern side is actually 19th century; the left-hand wing now houses the multi-media experience "Historium" *(see p94)*. The Markt is also the site of a large market on Wednesday mornings, and the Christmas market (with an ice rink taking centre stage) in December.

2 Belfort
MAP K4 ■ Markt 7 ■ Open 9:30am–6pm daily (last entry 5pm) ■ Adm

For a breathtaking view over Bruges' medieval streets, climb the 366 steps to the top of the Belfort (belfry). The set of bells at the top includes the 47 carillon bells that are rung by a mechanism installed in 1748. But they can also be played manually from a keyboard on the floor below by the town's *beiaardier* (carillon player) – Bruges' highest paid official, as the joke goes.

3 The Burg

This intimate and fetching square – a glittering confection of historic architecture, sculpture and gilding – was the focal point of old Bruges *(see pp28–9)*.

4 Steenhouwersdijk and Groenerei
MAP L4

Just south of the Burg is one of the prettiest stretches of canal, where calm waters reflect the medieval bridges and skyline. Here, the Steenhouwersdijk (stonemason's embankment) becomes the Groenerei (green canal) and is flanked by a picturesque almshouse called De Pelikaan, dated 1714 and named after the symbol of Christian charity, the pelican.

The canal from Steenhouwersdijk

5 Groeningemuseum

Not only is this one of the great northern European collections, with star roles played by the late medieval masters of Flemish painting, such as Jan van Eyck and Hans Memling; it is also refreshingly compact *(see pp30–31)*.

6 Sint-Janshospitaal

Hans Memling (c. 1430–94) was one of the leading artists of Burgundian Flanders, and the St John's Hospital ranked among his most important patrons. Visitors are advised to use the excellent audioguides available with the entry ticket. The medieval hospital wards display a fascinating miscellany of treasures, paintings and historic medical equipment; there is also a 15th-century pharmacy. The exhibition culminates in the chapel, which contains the hospital's priceless collection of Memling paintings (see pp30–31).

7 Onze-Lieve-Vrouwekerk

MAP K5 ▪ Mariastraat ▪ Open 9:30am–5pm Mon–Sat, 1:30pm–5pm Sun ▪ Adm for museum (church free)

The towering spire of the Church of Our Lady (the tallest structure in the city) is another key landmark of Bruges' skyline. It's a strange architectural mishmash: the exterior is a good example of the rather austere style known as Scheldt Gothic, and was built over two centuries from 1220 onward. The interior is essentially Gothic, with Baroque flourishes to its statues and extravagant pulpit (1743). This is a rather surprising setting for one of the great treasures of northern Europe:

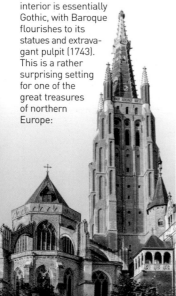

Michelangelo's *Madonna and Child* (1504–5) – a Carrara marble statue that came here by virtue of Bruges' close links to Renaissance Italy, and the only sculpture by Michelangelo to leave Italy during his lifetime. The church's museum includes the beautiful gilt-brass tombs of Charles the Bold (1433–77), Duke of Burgundy, and his daughter Mary (1457–82). Extensive renovation work (taking place until 2018) means some artifacts may be out of view.

8 Arentshuis

MAP K4 ▪ Dijver 16 ▪ Open 9:30am–5pm Tue–Sun ▪ Adm charge

Born in Bruges, the gifted painter Frank Brangwyn (1867–1956) was the son of William Curtis Brangwyn, one of a group of British artists and architects involved in restoring the city to its Gothic glory. Frank Brangwyn donated an impressive, small, collection of his work to the city. It is now exhibited on the upper floor of the late-18th-century Arentshuis building. The ground floor is used for temporary exhibitions.

Onze-Lieve-Vrouwekerk

⑨ Gruuthusemuseum
MAP K4 ■ Dijver 17 ■ **Closed for renovation until the end of 2017**

If it is hard to picture quite how life was led during Bruges' past, this museum will do much to fill in the gaps. It presents a rich collection of everyday artifacts from the homes of the merchant classes, from kitchenware to musical instruments, furniture and textiles, and even weapons. The 15th-century building was once the palace of the Lords of Gruuthuse, who became wealthy through a tax on beer flavourings (*gruut*); as a mark of their status, the house has a gallery overlooking the choir of the Onze-Lieve Vrouwekerk next door. The house was restored in the 19th century to exhibit the pieces that founded this collection.

Gruuthusemuseum

⑩ Begijnhof
MAP K5 ■ Wijngaardstraat
■ Grounds open 6:30am–6:30pm daily; Begijnhuisje open 10am–5pm
■ Adm to Begijnhuisje (grounds free)

This beautiful enclave was home to a community of *béguines* (*see box*) from 1245 until 1928, and expresses something essential about the soul of Bruges. Around the peaceful, tree-shaded park are the 17th- and 18th-century whitewashed homes of the *béguines*, and now occupied by Benedictine nuns. You can visit the grounds, the *béguinage* church and one of the houses (Begijnhuisje).

A DAY IN BRUGES

▶ **MORNING**

A day of wandering. Begin in the **Burg** (*see pp28–9*) and head south across Blinde Ezelstraat. Linger beside the canals on **Steenhouwersdijk** and **Groenerei** (*see p91*); walk through Huidenvettersplein to the **Dijver** for the prettiest views of the city. Now make your way past **Onze-Lieve-Vrouwekerk** to **Mariastraat** and **Katelijnestraat**, where you could stop for a divine hot chocolate at **De Proeverie** (*see p97*). Take Wijngaardstraat to the **Begijnhof**, loop around the **Minnewater** (*see p94*), and go back along Katelijnestraat. Note the almshouses that pop up on this street (for instance at Nos 87–101 and 79–83). For lunch, try the **Vismarkt** area – Wijnbar Est, for example (*see p97*).

AFTERNOON

Now you are going to pass through the city's medieval trading centre. From the **Markt** (*see p91*) walk up Vlamingstraat. At **Beursplein**, there was a cluster of national "lodges" – headquarters of foreign traders – such as the **Genoese Lodge** (No 33). One of Bruge's more unusual attractions is on Vlamingstraat: the **Frietmuseum** (*see p94*) is dedicated to *frites*. Then walk up Langerei to follow the canal that leads to **Damme** (*see p69*), where goods were transferred from ships to canal barges. Head back down Sint-Jakobstraat, and take a detour to **'t Brugs Beertje** (*see p97*), with its famed beers.

See map on p90 ←

The Best of the Rest

1 Sint-Salvatorskathedraal

MAP K4 ■ Steenstraat ■ Open 10am–1pm & 2–5:30pm (til 3:30pm Sat) Mon–Sat, 11:30am–12pm & 2–5pm Sun

It was at St Saviour's that the Order of the Golden Fleece met in 1478.

2 Sint-Walburgakerk

MAP L3 ■ Sint-Maartensplein ■ Open 10am–1pm & 2–6pm daily

This handsome Jesuit church, built in 1619–43, is a Baroque symphony in black-and-white marble, with a supreme wooden pulpit.

3 Godshuis De Vos

MAP K5 ■ Noordstraat 2–8

The almshouses (godshuizen) of Bruges are easily identified by their humble whitewashed walls, inscribed with names and dates. This delightful example dates from 1643.

4 Minnewater

MAP K6

Romantic, willow-lined lake formed by a sluice gate on the River Reie – a hectic port in medieval times.

Swans on Minnewater lake

5 Diamantmuseum

MAP K5 ■ Katelijnestraat 43 ■ 050 34 20 56 ■ Open 10:30am–5:30pm daily ■ Closed 2nd & 3rd weeks Jan ■ Adm ■ www.diamond museum.be

The history of diamonds explained.

Huisbrouwerij De Halve Maan

6 Huisbrouwerij De Halve Maan

MAP K5 ■ Walplein 26 ■ 050 44 42 22 ■ Tours 11am–4pm daily (to 5pm Sat) ■ Adm ■ www.halvemaan.be

Follow the beer-making process at this brewery, in operation since 1856.

7 Frietmuseum

MAP K3 ■ Vlamingstraat 33 ■ 050 34 01 50 ■ Open 10am–5pm daily ■ Adm ■ www.frietmuseum.be

This unusual museum is dedicated to the Belgian's adored frites.

8 Choco-Story

MAP L3 ■ Wijnzakstraat 2 ■ 050 61 22 37 ■ Open 10am–5pm daily ■ Adm ■ www. choco-story-brugge.be

This converted 15th-century taverne educates visitors on the production of famous Belgian chocolate.

9 Historium

MAP K4 ■ Markt 1 ■ 050 27 03 11 ■ Open 10am–6pm daily ■ Adm ■ www.historium.be

A multi-media experience evoking the medieval Golden Age of Bruges through a tale of young romance.

10 Sint-Jakobskerk

MAP K3 ■ Open Jul–Aug only: 2–5:30pm Mon–Fri & Sun, 2–4pm Sat

The church of St James is Bruges' richest parish church and contains notable paintings and tombs.

See map on p90

Eastern Bruges: Sint-Anna

1 Onze-Lieve-Vrouw ter Potterie

MAP L1 ▪ Potterierei 79 ▪ Open 9:30am–12:30pm, 1:30–5pm Tue–Sun ▪ Adm

This charming little museum combines treasures, oddities and an elaborate Baroque chapel.

2 Duinenbrug

MAP L2

Bruges' canals were spanned by charming little drawbridges to allow boats to pass. This one is a reconstruction from 1976.

3 Volkskundemuseum

MAP L3 ▪ Balstraat 43 ▪ Open 9:30am–5pm Tue–Sun ▪ Adm

Occupying eight 17th-century almshouses in the east of the city, Bruges' folk museum presents a fascinating collection of historic artifacts through life-size dioramas.

4 Sint-Annakerk

MAP L3 ▪ Open 10am–1pm & 2pm–6pm daily

Dominating a tiny square, Sint-Annakerk was elegantly refurbished after destruction by the iconoclasts. The austere building is a tranquil place of worship enlivened by Baroque flourishes.

5 Gezellemuseum

MAP M2 ▪ Rolweg 64 ▪ Open 9:30am–12:30pm & 1:30–5pm Tue–Sun ▪ Adm

Rustic home of one of the best-loved poets in Dutch (and Flemish), the priest Guido Gezelle (1830–99).

6 Schuttersgilde Sint-Sebastiaan

MAP M2 ▪ Carmersstraat 174 ▪ 050 33 16 26 ▪ Open Apr–Sep: 10am–noon Tue–Thu, 2–5pm Sat; Oct–Mar: 2–5pm Tue–Thu & Sat ▪ Adm

This historic archers' guildhouse still functions as an archery club.

7 Jeruzalemkapel

MAP L3 ▪ Peperstraat 3 ▪ 050 33 88 83 ▪ Open 10am–5pm Mon–Sat ▪ Adm ▪ www.adornes.org

A real curiosity – a 15th-century private chapel inspired by pilgrimages to Jerusalem. Next door is the Kantcentrum (Lace Centre).

8 Windmills on the Kruisvest

MAP M2 ▪ Open 9:30am–12:30pm & 1:30–5pm Tue–Sun (Sint-Janshuismolen: Apr–Sep; Koeleweimolen: Jul & Aug) ▪ Adm

Two of the city's four remaining working flour windmills – Sint-Janshuismolen and Koeleweimolen – are open to the public.

9 Kantcentrum

MAP L3 ▪ Balstraat 16 ▪ 050 33 00 72 ▪ Open Apr–Sep: 9.30–5pm ▪ Adm ▪ www.kantcentrum.eu

The Lace Centre explains the history of Bruges' lace, with live demonstrations in the afternoon (Mon–Sat).

10 Kruispoort

MAP M3

One of only four surviving gates of the city walls.

Kruispoort

Shopping

1 Steenstraat and Zuidzandstraat
MAP K4

The main shopping area links the Markt to 't Zand. Clothes, shoes, chocolates – they're all here.

Shoppers on Steenstraat

2 Zilverpand
MAP K4

This warren of arcades between Zuidzandstraat and Noordzandstraat consists mainly of clothes boutiques.

3 Sukerbuyc
MAP K5 ▪ Katelijnestraat 5

There are chocolate shops at every turn in Bruges, but "Sugarbelly" is family-run and the cocoa treats are handmade on site.

4 The Bottle Shop
MAP K4 ▪ Wollestraat 13

Bruges' own brewery De Halve Maan (see p 94) produces two beers, Brugse Zot and Straffe Hendrik. You can find them here, along with the full Belgian range.

5 't Apostolientje
MAP L3 ▪ Balstraat 11

There are still some lacemakers in Bruges, though not the 10,000 there were in 1840. A number of lace shops line Breidelstraat between the Markt and the Burg, but this one is the most authentic.

Knick-knacks for sale at a market

6 2be
MAP L4 ▪ Wollestraat 53

This shop in a converted 15th-century mayor's house stocks beers, chocolate and biscuits. The bar upstairs offers good canal views.

7 Huis Van Loocke
MAP L4 ▪ Ezelstraat 17
▪ Closed Sun & Mon morning

Bruges attracts many artists, and several excellent shops cater to their needs. This one has been run by the same family for three generations.

8 Pollentier-Maréchal
MAP K5 ▪ Sint-Salvatorskerkhof 8 ▪ Closed Sun & Mon

This fine shop sells old prints, many of them of Bruges.

9 Supermarkets
MAP M3 ▪ Langestraat 55

The major supermarkets (such as Louis Delhaize) are in the suburbs, but a few small ones, such as Smatch, lie within the city.

10 Markets
MAP J4, K4, L4

General markets are in the Markt (Wednesday mornings) and on 't Zand (Saturday mornings). The Christmas market takes place in the Markt and Simon Stevinplein. Flea markets are held weekend afternoons on Dijver and at the Vismarkt.

Cafés, Tearooms and Bars

Funky interior of Duvelorium, run by Belgian brewery Duvel

1 De Garre
MAP K4 = De Garre 1 (off Breidelstraat)

A well-known old *staminee* (pub), hidden down an alleyway. Famous for its strong 11% beer.

2 Café Vlissinghe
MAP L3 = Blekerstraat 2
= Closed Mon & Tue

This is said to be the oldest Bruges tavern, founded in 1515. Van Dyck apparently met local painters here. There's a boules court outside and light lunches are served.

3 De Proeverie
MAP K5 = Katelijnestraat 6
= Closed Mon

This delightful little coffee shop belongs to the chocolatier opposite: hot chocolate is a speciality.

4 Yesterday's World
MAP K5 = Wijngaardstraat 6

Splendidly quirky pub and cafe, close to the Begijnhof, full of antiques and bric-a-brac for sale.

5 Wijnbar Est
MAP L4 = Braambergstraat 7
= 050 33 38 39 = Closed Tue–Thu

A tiny, red-brick house that backs onto the canal with live jazz every Sunday from 8pm. Serves snacks and an excellent selection of wines.

6 Duvelorium
MAP K4 = Markt 1
= 050 27 03 11 = Open 11am–6pm

Part of the Historium (*see p 94*), showcasing Belgian beers, with a balcony terrace on the Markt.

7 Joey's Café
MAP K4 = Zilversteeg 4 (off Zuidzandstraat) 16a = 050 34 12 64
= Closed Sun

A fun café-bar with low-lit tables, comfy chairs and friendly staff. Hosts occasional free concerts.

8 't Brugs Beertje
MAP K4 = Kemelstraat 5
= Closed Wed

One of the great beer pubs, serving no fewer than 300 types of beer, including local brews Brugse Zot and Straffe Hendrik.

9 The Vintage
MAP K5 = Westmeers 13
= 050 34 30 63= Closed Wed

This lively bar decorated with vintage paraphernalia is located just around the corner from 't Zand tourist information centre.

10 De Republiek
MAP K3 = Sint-Jakobstraat 36
= 050 73 47 64

A large, time-worn bar where the young staff create a vibrant atmosphere. Good for cocktails too.

See map on p90

Restaurants

(1) De Karmeliet
MAP L3 ■ Langestraat 19
■ 050 33 82 59 ■ Closed Sun, Mon,
Tue L Jan & late Jun–mid-Jul ■ €€€
With three Michelin stars to its
name, this is one of Belgium's top
restaurants. Exquisite.

(2) De Stoepa
MAP K5 ■ Oostmeers 124
■ 050 33 04 54 ■ Closed Mon ■ €
Head to this Mediterranean-style
café to enjoy lunch from a good
menu of tapas, salads and soups.
There's a leafy summer terrace.

(3) Den Gouden Harynck
MAP L5 ■ Groeninge 25
■ 050 33 76 37 ■ Closed Sun, Mon &
last two weeks Jul ■ €€€
Housed in an attractive 17th-century
house, this is one of Bruges' finest
restaurants. Book ahead.

(4) Den Gouden Karpel
MAP L4 ■ Huidenvettersplein 4
■ 050 33 34 94 ■ Closed Mon ■ €€€
A fine fish restaurant beside the
Vismarkt (fish market), with an
excellent fish-shop/*traiteur* next door.

(5) Bistro de Schaar
MAP M4 ■ Hooistraat 2 ■ 050
33 59 79 ■ Closed Wed & Thu ■ €€
This snug restaurant is renowned for
its steaks grilled over an open fire
and its homemade desserts.

De Karmeliet offers high-end dining

(6) Rock Fort
MAP L3 ■ Langestraat 15 ■ 050
33 41 13 ■ Closed Sat & Sun ■ €€€
Pared-down modern interior in
an old family house. The two
young owners bring flair to the
contemporary cuisine.

(7) Assiette Blanche
MAP L4 ■ Philipstockstraat
23–5 ■ 050 34 00 94 ■ Closed Tue
& Wed ■ €€€
Exciting, inventive two-, three-
or four-course menus, with each
course designed to match an
accompanying beer.

(8) Den Amand
MAP K4 ■ Sint-Amandsstraat 4
■ 050 34 01 22 ■ Closed Sun & Wed
■ €€
A small restaurant serving inventive
dishes of worldwide inspiration.

(9) Marieke van Brugghe
MAP K4 ■ Mariastraat 17 ■ 050
34 33 66 ■ Closed Sun eve & Mon ■ €€
Dine beneath a replica panel from
the Sistine Chapel at this cosy bistro
that serves good beer-soaked stews.

(10) Patrick Devos
MAP K4 ■ Zilverstraat 41
■ 050 33 55 66 ■ Closed Wed D, Sat L,
Sun ■ €€€
An elegant restaurant cherished for
chef Patrick Devos' creative touch.

Belle-époque style at Patrick Devos

Lunch Spots, Bistros, Brasseries

PRICE CATEGORIES

For a three-course meal for one with half a bottle of wine (or equivalent meal), taxes and extra charges.

€ under €40   €€ €40–60   €€€ over €60

1 Bistro de Pompe
MAP K4 ■ Kleine Sint-Amandstraat 2 ■ 050 61 66 18 ■ Closed Sun D, Mon ■ €€

This very popular bistro serves an excellent-value weekday lunch menu. On offer are hearty meals and salads. Intimate relaxed atmosphere.

Elegant Bistro Christophe

2 Bistro Christophe
MAP L5 ■ Garenmarkt 34 ■ 050 34 48 92 ■ Closed lunch, Tue & Wed ■ €€€

Lovely little bistro, which is favoured by locals, serving well-judged Belgian-French cuisine.

3 Het Dagelijks Brood
MAP K4 ■ Philipstockstraat 21 ■ €

Or "Le Pain Quotidien" in French, this café is part of a chain providing wholesome sandwiches on crusty bread, plus pâtisserie and other snacks.

4 Pas Partout
MAP L4 ■ Kruitenbergstraat 11 ■ 050 33 51 16 ■ Closed Sun ■ €

Set up to provide inexpensive food for those who need it, Pas Partout also takes on unemployed individuals as chefs to learn a new trade. They serve the cheapest *steak frites* in town.

5 De Belegde Boterham
MAP K4 ■ Kleine Sint-Amandsstraat 5 ■ 050 34 91 31 ■ Closed Sun ■ €

A minimalist "lunch boutique" specialising in open sandwiches along with soups, salads and cakes.

6 Salade Folle
MAP K5 ■ Walplein 13–14 ■ 0474 36 25 33 ■ Closed Sun & Mon ■ €

A deservedly popular lunch spot and tearoom serving light, mainly vegetarian dishes, including soups, salads, and homemade cakes.

7 Lotus
MAP L4 ■ Wapenmakersstraat 5 ■ Open 11:30am–2pm Mon–Sat ■ €

This lovely vegetarian café is housed in the former residence of prolific painter Jacob van Oost.

8 Blackbird
MAP L3 ■ Jan van Eyckplein 7 ■ 050 34 74 44 ■ Closed Mon ■ €

An elegant, charming and health-conscious spot for breakfast, lunch and tea, particularly noted for its wholesome salads and sandwiches.

9 In't Nieuw Museum
MAP M4 ■ Hooistraat 42 ■ 050 33 12 80 ■ Closed Wed ■ €€

In this old family-run tavern, the meat is cooked on an open fire (evenings) in a 17th-century fireplace. The atmosphere is traditional and very friendly.

10 Gran Kaffee de Passage
MAP K4 ■ Dweersstraat 26 ■ 050 34 02 32 ■ Closed Mon ■ €

A wonderful dark-wood dining room lit mainly by candles is the setting for this restaurant. Gran Kaffee is highly respected for its solid, good-value Belgian dishes.

See map on p90

TOP 10 Antwerp

Exhibit, Museum Aan de Stroom

Set on the Broad River Scheldt, at the gateway to the North Sea, Antwerp is one of the leading trading cities of northern Europe; and in the early 17th century it was one of the great cultural centres too. The city has had its share of suffering – battered by the religious wars of the 16th century, cut off from the North Sea by treaty with the Netherlands from 1648 to 1795, and bombed in World War II. These historical ups and downs have endowed the city with a keen edge, like its famous diamonds. This dynamic energy is seen today in its hip bars, restaurants and nightclubs.

AREA MAP OF ANTWERP

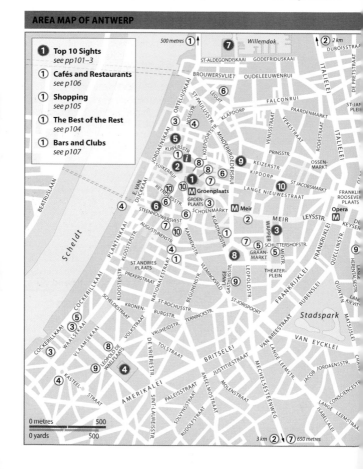

Grote Markt with its central fountain

① Onze-Lieve-Vrouwekathedraal

This huge Gothic cathedral, a city landmark, contains several splendid works by Rubens (see pp32–3).

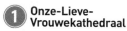

② Grote Markt

MAP T1 ▪ Stadhuis: guided tours only, book three weeks ahead (ask at tourist office, Grote Markt 13, 03 232 01 03; tour in English 2pm Sun) ▪ Adm

The main square of Antwerp is one of the great gilded arenas of Belgium. The city authorities made a virtue of its unusual "dog-leg" shape and slope by commissioning sculptor Jef Lambeaux (1852–1908) to create an eye-catching fountain, placed off-centre, with its water spilling out onto the cobbles. It depicts Brabo, a legendary Roman soldier who freed the port of Antwerp by defeating the giant Antigoon and throwing his severed hand (hand-werpen) into the river. The Italian-influenced Stadhuis (town hall) dominates the square. Built in the 1560s, its grand horizontals are offset by the upward curve of the roof-corners.

③ Rubenshuis

A rare chance not only to visit the house and studio of one of the great stars of European art, but also to see what a 17th-century patrician home looked like (see pp34–5).

View from the gardens, Rubenshuis

④ Koninklijk Museum voor Schone Kunsten (KMSKA)

MAP S3 ▪ Leopold de Waelplaats ▪ 03 224 95 50 ▪ www.kmska.be

Antwerp's fine arts museum is second only to Brussels' with its full range of paintings, from early Flemish "Primitives" to the Symbolists. The Neo-Classical building is undergoing an extensive renovation until late 2018. For more information visit the website.

Museum Vleeshuis

> **THE RIVER SCHELDT**
>
> Old Antwerp lies on the east bank of the River Scheldt (or Schelde). The river is so broad that the modern suburb on the west bank seems utterly remote (it is linked by tunnels). The Scheldt is deep enough to bring large ships to Antwerp's docks to the north of the city. This easy access to the North Sea has made Antwerp Europe's second-largest port.

⑤ Museum Vleeshuis

MAP T1 ▪ Vleeshouwersstraat 38 ▪ 03 292 61 00 ▪ Open 10am–5pm Thu–Sun ▪ Adm ▪ www. museumvleeshuis.be

With its turrets and towers and Gothic detail, the "Meat House" is one of the most beautiful buildings of Antwerp. Built in 1501–4 as the guildhouse of the butchers and a meat market, it is now used as a museum of music. The Museum Vleeshuis charts the history of the city through its many forms of musical expression, using historical instruments, including harpsichords made by the famous Ruckers family, manuscripts and a bell foundry.

⑥ Museum Plantin-Moretus

MAP T2 ▪ Vrijdagmarkt 22 ▪ 03 221 14 50 ▪ Open 10am–5pm Tue–Sun; closed public hols ▪ Adm (free last Wed of month) ▪ www.museumplantinmoretus.be

Christopher Plantin (c.1520–89) was a French bookbinder who, in 1546, came to Antwerp to set up his own printing workshop. It became one of the most influential publishing houses in Europe during the late Renaissance, producing Bibles, maps, scientific books and much more. The museum consists essentially of the printing workshop and home of Plantin and his heirs. It contains a large collection of rare and precious books, and displays of their illustrations.

⑦ Museum Aan de Stroom (MAS)

MAP T1 ▪ Hanzestedenplaats 1 ▪ 03 338 44 00 ▪ Open Apr–Oct: 10am–5pm Tue–Fri & 10am–6pm Sat & Sun; Nov–Mar: 10am–5pm Tue–Sun; closed pub hols ▪ Adm (free last Wed of month) ▪ www.mas.be

It is impossible to miss this towering dockside museum built of red sandstone and perspex. It uses the city's collection of ethnographic and folkloric treasures to explore mankind and our interaction with the world.

⑧ Museum Mayer van den Bergh

MAP T2 ▪ Lange Gasthuisstraat 19 ▪ 03 338 81 88 ▪ Open 10am–5pm Tue–Sun ▪ Adm (free last Wed of month) ▪ www. museummayervandenbergh.be

Fritz Mayer van den Bergh (1858–91) was an avid collector of art and curios. When he died, his mother

Museum Mayer van den Bergh

created a museum to display his collections – some 5,000 items in all. They include tapestries, furniture, stained glass, paintings and coins.

⑨ Rockoxhuis
MAP U1 ■ **Keizerstraat 10–12**
■ **03 201 92 50** ■ **Open 10am–5pm Tue–Sun** ■ **Adm (free last Wed of month)** ■ **www.rockoxhuis.be**

Come here for a glimpse of the grace and elegance of 17th-century patrician style. A series of rooms contains a fine collection of furniture, paintings and artifacts. The house is named after its owner, city mayor Nicholas Rockox (1560–1640), a philanthropist and a friend and patron of Rubens. There are paintings and drawings by Rubens, Jordaens and Van Dyck, as well as work by painter Frans Snyders (1579–1657), who lived next door.

Stained-glass detail, Sint-Jacobskerk

⑩ Sint-Jacobskerk
MAP U2 ■ **Lange Nieuwstraat 73–75** ■ **048 605 54 39** ■ **Open 1 Apr–31 Oct: 2–5pm daily** ■ **Adm**

Of all the churches in Antwerp, the church of St James is noted for having the richest interior – and for being the burial place of Rubens. It was built in late Gothic style in the 15th and 16th centuries by architects who also worked on the cathedral. The church contains work by leading sculptors of the 17th century, such as Lucas Faydherbe and Hendrik Verbruggen, as well as paintings by Rubens, Jordaens and Van Dyck.

A DAY IN ANTWERP

▶ MORNING

This day of gentle ambling takes in many of the key sights of Antwerp, as well as some of the best shopping streets. Start off at the **Museum Vleeshuis** and head for the old city centre – the **Grote Markt** (see p101) – and the **cathedral** (see pp32–3). Thread your way to Wijngaardstraat, and the fetching ensemble of the **Sint-Carolus Borromeuskerk** (see p104), before heading on to the **Rockoxhuis** in Keizerstraat. After this, walk south along Katelijnevest to the **Meir**. The tower block to your right, with KBC on its crest, is the **Boerentoren**, the highest building in Europe when constructed in 1932. Head down the Meir to the **Rubenshuis** (see pp34–5); you can lunch here, or if you prefer at the **Grand Café Horta** (see p106).

AFTERNOON

Now you've done the culture, you can wander the neighbourhood's shopping streets (see p105). **Schuttershofstraat** is a good place to start. It leads to Huidevettersstraat, the Nieuwe Gaanderij Arcade, Korte Gasthuisstraat and Lombardenvest. If you are in the mood for more museums, the excellent **Museum Mayer van den Bergh** and the **Maagdenhuismuseum** (see p104) are just to the south. Or head for Nationalestraat and Dries van Noten's outlet, the beautiful **Het Modepaleis**, (see p105), and then down to **Dock's Café** (see p106) or **De Vagant** (see p107) for refreshment.

See map on pp100–101 ←

The Best of the Rest

Red Star Line Museum exhibits

1 Red Star Line Museum
MAP T1 ▪ Montevideostraat 3
▪ 03 298 27 70 ▪ Open 10am–5pm
Tue–Sun; closed public hols ▪ Adm
▪ www.redstarline.be

Between 1873 and 1934, Red Star ocean liners departed from Antwerp's docks for the United States, taking families to a new life. This museum explores their journey.

2 Middelheim Museum
Middelheimlaan 61 ▪ 03 288
33 60 ▪ Open 10am–dusk Mon–Sat;
closed public hols

High-quality open-air sculpture park, with hundreds of modern and contemporary pieces.

3 FotoMuseum Provincie Antwerpen (FoMU)
MAP S3 ▪ Waalsekaai 47 ▪ 03 242
93 00 ▪ Open 10am–6pm Tue–
Sun ▪ Adm ▪ www.
fotomuseum.be

Antwerp's excellent museum of photography and historical artifacts has ever-changing exhibitions.

4 Sint-Pauluskerk
MAP T1 ▪ Veemarkt 13
▪ 03 232 32 67 ▪ Open 1
Apr–31 Oct: 2–5pm daily

Gothic and Baroque fight it out over the exterior of this endearing church.

5 MUHKA
MAP S3 ▪ Leuvenstraat 32
▪ 03 260 99 99 ▪ Open 11am–6pm
Tue–Sun (11am–9pm Thu); closed
public hols ▪ Adm ▪ www.muhka.be

A former warehouse is home to the cutting-edge Museum van Hedendaagse Kunst, which is all about contemporary art.

6 Sint-Carolus Borromeuskerk
MAP T1 ▪ Hendrik Conscienceplein 6
▪ 03 231 37 51 ▪ Open 10am–
12:30pm, 2–5pm Mon–Sat;
for religious services Sun

This church is renowned for its Baroque façade and its tragic loss of 39 Rubens' paintings.

7 De Koninck Brewery
Mechelsesteenweg 291
▪ 03 866 96 90 ▪ Open 10am–6pm
Tue–Sun (last entry 4:30pm) ▪ Adm
▪ www.dekoninck.be

Visitor centre and tours at Antwerp's most famous brewery.

8 Cogels-Osylei
In the late 19th century, this area became a showcase for opulent architecture – some of the examples are quite extraordinary.

9 Maagdenhuismuseum
MAP T3 ▪ Lange Gasthuisstraat
33 ▪ 03 338 26 20 ▪ Open 10am–5pm
Mon, Wed–Fri, 1–5pm Sat–Sun;
closed public hols ▪ Adm

This quirky museum, with some lovely old masters, is set in an old orphanage.

**Porridge bowl,
Maagdenhuismuseum**

10 ModeMuseum MoMu
MAP T2 ▪ Nationalestraat
28 ▪ 03 470 27 70
▪ Open 10am–6pm Tue–Sun
▪ Adm ▪ www.momu.be

A museum of *haute couture* presenting fashion in its social, political and cultural context.

Shopping

1 **Nieuwe Gaanderij Arcade**
MAP T2 ■ **Between Huidevettersstraat and Korte Gasthuisstraat**
A good place to seek out fashion at a slightly lower price than the usual designer boutiques.

Meir, busy with shoppers

2 **Meir**
MAP U2
The main shopping street is a broad pedestrianized avenue, fronted largely by high-street chain stores.

3 **Grand Bazar Shopping Center**
MAP T2 ■ **Beddenstraat 2**
An elegant modern arcade shares space with the Hilton hotel in the shell of a former department store.

4 **Nationalestraat**
MAP T2
The heart of Antwerp's *haute-couture* fashion district offers boutiques by many world-class designers but remains accessible to all.

5 **Schuttershofstraat**
MAP U3
Another street of recherché boutiques and shoe shops, including a branch of the ultimate Belgian accessories manufacturer Delvaux. You can smell the leather!

6 **Het Modepaleis**
MAP T2 ■ **Nationalestraat 16**
This elegant *belle époque* "flat iron" building is the main outlet for one of Antwerp's most fêted fashion designers, Dries van Noten.

7 **DVS**
MAP U2 ■ **Schuttershofstraat 9 (first floor)**
A fashion boutique set up by Dirk Saene (one of the famous "Antwerp Six") and carrying work by other Antwerp luminaries, including Walter Van Beirendonck, Veronique Branquinho and Raf Simons.

8 **Ann Demeulemeester**
MAP S3 ■ **Leopold de Waelplaats/Verlatstraat**
Only a short distance from the MUHKA contemporary art gallery, Demeulemeester's shop displays the uncompromising edge that has placed her at the forefront of fashion.

9 **Diamondland**
MAP V2 ■ **Appelmansstraat 33A**
Diamonds at lower prices than elsewhere in Europe. At the same time as purchasing that special ring, you can learn about diamonds.

A sparkling window display, Meir

10 **Pelikaanstraat**
MAP V2
Wall-to-wall diamond and jewellery shops in the Jewish quarter. Fascinating, partly because there's nothing romantic about it – the gems are commodities like any other.

See map on pp100–101 ←

Cafés and Restaurants

① Huis de Colvenier
MAP T2 ▪ Sint-Antoniusstraat 8
▪ 0477 23 26 50 ▪ Closed Sun, Mon
▪ €€€

This is one of the most respected restaurants in Antwerp, so you should book in advance.

② Den Abattoir
Lange Lobroekstraat 65 ▪ 03 271 08 71 ▪ Closed Sat L ▪ €€

Located next to Park Spoor Noord, this former slaughterhouse dishes up ultra-fresh steak and ribs.

③ Dock's Café
MAP T1 ▪ Jordaenskaai 7
▪ 03 226 63 30 ▪ Closed Sun ▪ €€

Renowned for its oysters and its inventive, multi-layered interior by celebrated designer Antoine Pinto.

④ Restaurant aan de Stroom
MAP T2 ▪ Ernest van Dijckkaai 37
▪ 03 234 12 75 ▪ €€

A landmark building looming over the River Scheldt. Home to an elegant, first-class brasserie.

⑤ Grand Café Horta
MAP U2 ▪ Hopland 2
▪ 03 203 56 60 ▪ €€

A dynamic space created using metal salvaged from Victor Horta's celebrated Art Nouveau Volkshuis (Brussels), demolished in 1965.

Courtyard, De Groote Witte Arrend

⑥ De Groote Witte Arrend
MAP T2 ▪ Reyndersstraat 18
▪ 03 233 50 33 ▪ €€

A celebrated old-world tavern in a grand 17th-century convent, with its own chapel. It serves a good range of Flemish food and beers.

⑦ Günther Watté
MAP T2 ▪ Steenhouwersvest 30 ▪ 03 293 58 94 ▪ Closed Mon ▪ €

With its renowned pralines made in-house, this café is a favourite with connoisseurs of coffee and chocolate.

⑧ Het Vermoeide Model
MAP T2 ▪ Lijnwaadmarkt 2
▪ 03 233 52 61 ▪ Closed Mon ▪ €€

This brasserie-restaurant creates an intimate mood with medieval beams, and has an outdoor terrace.

⑨ Dôme Sur Mer
Arendstraat 1 ▪ 03 281 74 33 ▪ Closed Sat L ▪ €€€

Floor-to-ceiling windows and a marble bar make an impressive setting for this hugely popular fish restaurant in the Zurenborg.

⑩ Brasserie Appelmans
MAP T2 ▪ Papenstraatje 1
▪ 03 226 20 22 ▪ €€

Inventive Belgian and international dishes among the brickwork of a beautifully renovated 19th-century building, with "Absinthbar".

Grand Café Horta interior

Bars and Clubs

PRICE CATEGORIES

For a three-course meal for one with half a bottle of wine (or equivalent meal), taxes and extra charges.

€ under €40 €€ €40–60 €€€ over €60

1 Den Engel
MAP T1 ■ Grote Markt 3
■ 03 233 12 52

A classic Belgian *bruine kroeg* (brown pub – brown with the patina of age) overlooking the Grote Markt. Try a *bolleke* (chalice-like glass) of De Koninck, Antwerp's own brew.

2 IKON
Kotterstraat 1 ■ 03 295 54 65

Take a taxi to this hip nightclub in the northern Het Eilandje district.

3 Café Local
MAP S3 ■ Waalsekaai 25
■ 03 500 03 67

A glamorous complex with themed Latin-American-style areas. It holds a salsa night on the first Sunday of the month.

Sips cocktail bar

4 Sips
Gillisplaats 8 ■ 0477 63 91 52

A chic cocktail bar in the arty dockland area south of the city centre. Cigars are a speciality.

5 D-Club
Damplein 27 ■ 0488 49 96 07

Predominantly gay nightclub with popular, free Saturday night parties.

6 Café d'Anvers
MAP T1 ■ Verversrui 15
■ 03 226 38 70

Antwerp's original nightclub is still one of the coolest. A great option if you want to listen to a mix of house, soul, disco and funk.

Chromatic lighting, Café d'Anvers

7 De Muze
MAP T2 ■ Melkmarkt 15
■ 03 226 01 26

A friendly pub where you can listen to live jazz most evenings until 2 or 3am. Exposed beams and brickwork create an intimate atmosphere.

8 Het Kathedraalcafé
MAP T1 ■ Torfbrug 10

Quirky, yet cosy, bar where the walls are packed with gaudy religious icons. A stairway to heaven?

9 Café Hopper
MAP S3 ■ Leopold de Waelstraat 2 ■ 03 248 49 33

This jazz bar, with live sessions several times a week, is very popular with Antwerp's creative set. Ask for a *"half en half"*: half cava; half white wine.

10 De Vagant
MAP T2 ■ Reyndersstraat 25
■ 03 233 15 38

A welcoming traditional café-bar offering some 200 types of *jenever* (gin). You can buy your favourite brand in the Slitterij shop upstairs.

See map on pp100–101 ←

📟 Ghent

Ghent has much in common with Bruges. It is a city with a rich legacy of medieval buildings and art treasures inherited from its days as a semi-autonomous and prosperous trading centre. The tranquil waters of its canals mirror the step-gables of its old guildhouses and the tall spires of its three famous towers. Unlike Bruges, however, historically prosperous Ghent took on a new lease of life as Belgium's first industrial city in the early 19th century. It is also home to a large university. These factors have endowed the city with a scale, bustle and youthful verve that have shaped its character. Ghent has a grandeur, symbolized by its cathedral, theatres and opera house, but it also has an intimacy, and the web of its medieval streets – including Europe's largest pedestrianized zone – makes this a perfect city for wandering.

AREA MAP OF GHENT

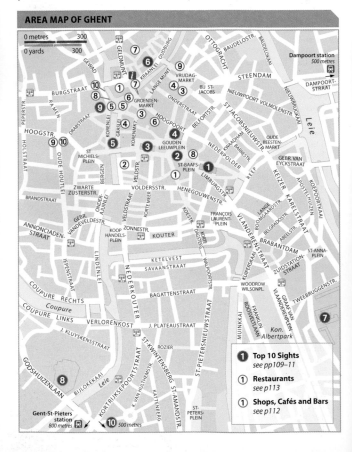

❶ **Top 10 Sights**
see pp109–11

① **Restaurants**
see p113

① **Shops, Cafés and Bars**
see p112

The stunning altar, Sint-Baafskathedraal

1 Sint-Baafskathedraal
MAP Q2 ■ Sint-Baafsplein
■ 09 269 20 45 ■ Open Apr–Oct:
8:30am–6pm Mon–Sat, 9:30am–6pm
Sun; Nov–Mar: 8:30am–5pm Mon–
Sat, 9:30am–5pm Sun (only
open to non- worshippers
after 1pm Sun) ■ Adm (Mystic
Lamb only)

St Bavo was a local 7th-
century saint. The
cathedral named after
him dates back to the
10th century, but most of
it is Gothic, built over
three centuries after
1290. Outstanding are the
grandiose Baroque-Rococo
pulpit of oak and marble (1741–5)
and the church's greatest treasure
the multi-panelled, 15th-century
altarpiece, The Adoration of the
Mystic Lamb by Hubrecht and Jan
van Eyck (see pp36–7).

2 Belfort
MAP Q2 ■ Sint-Baafsplein
■ 09 233 39 54 ■ Open 10am–6pm
daily ■ Adm

Ghent's belfry is a prominent
landmark, rising 91 m (299 ft) to
the gilded dragon on the tip of its
spire. It was built in 1380–81 and
served for centuries as look-out
tower, clock and alarm. It houses
a 54-bell carillon, which is used
for regular concerts. There is a
lift to transport visitors to the top.

3 Sint-Niklaaskerk
MAP Q2
■ Cataloniëstraat
■ Open 2–5pm Mon,
10am–5pm Tue–Sun

St Nicholas, Bishop of
Myra, was patron saint
of merchants, and this
was the merchants'
church. Built in the 13th
to 15th centuries, it is
Belgium's best example
of the austere style
called Scheldt Gothic.

4 Stadhuis
MAP Q2
■ Botermarkt 1 ■ Open May–
Sep: 2–4pm daily, book and depart
from Sint-Veerleplein tourist office
(Sat & Sun, includes tour of historical
centre and St Bavo's) ■ Adm

Standing on the main square
is the impressive town hall. It
has a series of regal council
chambers, still in use
today – some dating
back to the 15th century,
others refurbished
during restoration
after 1870.

Detail on the wall, Stadhuis

5 Graslei and Korenlei
MAP P2

The Graslei and Korenlei are departure points for canal trips. The two
quays are lined with the step-gabled
guildhouses of merchants and
tradesmen that date back to the
12th century. Sint-Michielsbrug,
the bridge at the southern end,
offers the best views of the city.

The quay, Graslei

Exhibit in the Huis van Alijn

6 Huis van Alijn

MAP Q1 ■ Kraanlei 65 ■ 09 235 38 00 ■ Open 11am–5:30pm Tue–Sat, 10am–5:30pm Sun ■ Adm

Just north of the centre of Ghent is a quaint and folksy quarter called the Patershol, a warren of little medieval streets and alleys (see p54). This is the backdrop for one of the best folk museums in Belgium. A huge and fascinating collection of artifacts – toys, games, shoes and crockery, as well as complete shops and craftsmen's workshops – are laid out within almshouses, which are set around a grassy courtyard. These almshouses were founded in 1363 as a children's hospital – not as an act of pure philanthropy but as penance for the murder of two members of the Alijn family.

7 Klein Begijnhof

MAP R4 ■ Lange Violettestraat 235 ■ Open 6:30am– 9:30pm daily

There are three béguinages (see p92) in Ghent, but this is by far the prettiest. With step-gabled, whitewashed houses set around a little park and Baroque church, it is a classic of its kind – a fact recognized by its status as a UNESCO World Heritage Site. It was founded as a community of single women in about 1235, and has been continuously occupied, although the residents are no longer béguines. Most of the present houses date from the 17th century.

8 STAM

MAP P4 ■ Godshuizenlaan 2 ■ 09 267 14 00 ■ Open 10am–6pm Tue–Sun ■ Adm ■ www.stamgent.be

The Abdij de Bijloke, an old rambling Cistercian convent and hospital, provides a superb setting for STAM, Ghent's City Museum. Covering the history of the city from prehistoric times to the present day, STAM incorporates the vast range of items of the former Bijloke Museum, including medieval tombs, free-masons' regalia and models of warships. The convent dates from medieval times, but most of the buildings are from the 17th century.

Antique map of Ghent, STAM

GHENT AND CHARLES V

Charles V (1500–58), Holy Roman Emperor, King of Spain, master of much of Europe and the New World, was born in Ghent, and his baptism in Sint-Baafskathedraal was celebrated with a huge feast. But the city's love affair with its famous son went sour when it found itself endlessly squeezed for taxes. A revolt in 1540, and the execution by hanging of its ringleaders, gave rise to the people of Ghent being called the *stroppendragers* ("noose bearers") – a proud symbol of their defiant and independent spirit.

9 Design Museum Gent

MAP P1 ▪ Jan Breydelstraat 5
▪ 09 267 99 99 ▪ Open 10am–6pm
Tue–Sun ▪ Adm ▪ www.
designmuseumgent.be

This museum is a must for anyone
with the slightest interest in
furniture, furnishings and interior
decoration. Housed in a grand
18th-century mansion, plus an
uncompromisingly modern
extension, it provides a tour through
changing European styles from the
17th century to the present. The Art
Nouveau collection is particularly
rewarding, with work by Horta, Paul
Hankar and René Lalique.

Exhibits, Design Museum Gent

10 Museum voor Schone Kunsten (MSK) and SMAK

MAP Q6 ▪ Citadelpark ▪ MSK: 09 240
07 00; www.mskgent.be; SMAK: 09
240 76 01; www.smak.be ▪ Open
10am–6pm Tue–Sun ▪ Adm

Ghent's two leading museums of art
are a short tram or bus ride south
of the city centre. The MSK (Fine Arts
Museum) covers painting and sculpture from the Middle Ages up to the
early 20th century and has a world-
class and eclectic collection of works
by a number of important artists, such
as Hieronymus Bosch, Rogier van der
Weyden and Hugo van der Goes.
Opposite the MSK is the Stedelijk
Museum voor Acktuele Kunst (SMAK),
Ghent's superb modern art gallery.
Its permanent collection – with pieces
by Magritte and Marcel Broodthaers –
and regularly changing temporary
exhibitions have placed SMAK at
the forefront of modern art galleries
in Europe.

A DAY IN GHENT

▶ MORNING

SMAK and the **Museum voor
Schone Kunsten** make a good
double act – a stimulating
mixture of fine art and pure
provocation, from world-class
artists. Get these under your belt
early in the day (note that they're
closed on Mon). Trams 1 and 10
run from the central Korenmarkt
to Charles de Kerchovelaan, from
where you can walk through or
beside the Citadelpark to the
museums. These will absorb the
greater part of the morning; you
can break for refreshments at
SMAK's café. For lunch, head
back into the city centre. The
Korenmarkt is equidistant from
two enticing and contrasting
lunch options: **The House of Eliott**
(see p113), and the medieval
Groot Vleeshuis (see p112).

AFTERNOON

Now go to **Sint-Baafskathedraal**
to see the **Mystic Lamb** (see
pp32–3). Then you can go up the
Belfort (see p109) to get a view
over the city. Now it's back to the
Korenmarkt, stopping off at the
Sint-Niklaaskerk (see p109), then
over to the **Graslei** and **Korenlei**
(see p109) to drink in the views.
This could be the time to take
a canal trip. From the Korenlei,
walk along Jan Breydelstraat and
take the first right into Rekelige-
straat to reach the **Gravensteen**
(Castle of the Counts). Then
cross the Zuivelbrug and
take Meerseniersstraat to the
Vrijdagmarkt (Friday Market) for
beer at **Dulle Griet** (see p112) and
chips at **Frituur Jozef** (see p113).

See map on p108

Shops, Cafés and Bars

1 Mageleinstraat and Koestraat
MAP Q2

Ghent city centre has an extensive pedestrianized zone, which makes shopping here all the more agreeable. Most chain stores are in Lange Munt and Veldstraat, but there's more charm around the quieter Mageleinstraat and Koestraat.

2 Markets
www.visitgent.be/en/markets

There is a market every day in Ghent (six on Sunday): a Sunday walking tour can take you to them all.

3 Tierenteyn-Verlent
MAP Q1 ■ Groentenmarkt 3 ■ Closed Sun

In situ since 1790, this delicatessen is famous for its homemade mustard that is pumped up from the cellars into a wooden barrel.

Herbs and spices, Tierenteyn-Verlent

4 Dulle Griet
MAP Q1 ■ Vrijdagmarkt 50

One of the celebrated "beer academies" of Belgium, with 250 beers on offer. Note the basket in which you must deposit a shoe as security when drinking Kwak, a beer served in its own unique glass.

5 Het Spijker
MAP P2 ■ Pensmarkt 3–5

Cosy candle-lit bar in the cellar of a 13th-century leprosy shelter, with a large, popular terrace.

Butcher's hall, Groot Vleeshuis

6 Groot Vleeshuis
MAP Q1 ■ Groentenmarkt 7 ■ 09 223 23 24 ■ Closed Mon ■ €

This centre for Eastern Flemish food – part restaurant, part delicatessen – is sensationally located in a medieval butchers' hall.

7 't Dreupelkot
MAP Q1 ■ Groentenmarkt 12

A waterfront bar serving only *jenever*, a form of gin, variously flavoured with fruit, vanilla and even chocolate.

8 Brooderie
MAP P1 ■ Jan Breydelstraat 8 ■ Closed Mon ■ €

The tempting smell of freshly baked bread wafts around this rustic-style eatery, which serves sandwiches and light vegetarian fare.

9 Hotsy Totsy
MAP P2 ■ Hoogstraat 1 ■ 09 224 20 12 ■ Closed Mon ■ €

Atmospheric 1930s decor and evenings of jazz, poetry and cabaret make this legendary Ghent bar worth seeking out.

10 Café Labath
MAP P2 ■ Oude Houtlei 1 ■ €

A popular locals café serving excellent coffee and hot chocolate, as well as delicous breakfasts, soups and sandwiches. Friendly service.

Restaurants

PRICE CATEGORIES
For a three-course meal for one with half
a bottle of wine (or equivalent meal),
taxes and extra charges
....
€ under €40   €€ €40–60   €€€ over €60

1 Oude Vismijn
MAP P1 ■ Sint-Veerleplein 5
■ 09 223 20 00 ■ Closed Mon ■ €€
Inside the renovated Fish Market,
this urbane brasserie's trump cards
are the stunning views of the Graslei
and Korenlei (see p109).

2 Brasserie Pakhuis
MAP P2 ■ Schuurkenstraat 4
■ 09 223 55 55 ■ Closed Sun ■ €€
Run by celebrated restaurant
designer Antoine Pinto, Pakhuis is
big and very popular – so reserve!

3 Keizershof
MAP Q1 ■ Vrijdagmarkt 47
■ 09 223 44 46 ■ Closed Sun, Mon
& Tue L ■ €€
A good list of mainly classic
Belgian dishes is served in this
lively brasserie, on several floors.

4 Belga Queen
MAP P2 ■ Graslei 10
■ 09 280 01 00 ■ €€€
The historic 13th-century building,
elegant decor and the quality of locally
sourced food create a high-end feel
within contemporary surroundings.

5 Korenlei Twee
MAP P2 ■ Korenlei 2 ■ 09 224
00 73 ■ Closed Sun D, Mon ■ €€€
This 18th-century dockside town
house, serves meals using
ingredients from the local fish
and meat markets. Good value
and excellent wine too.

6 Mosquito Coast
MAP Q2 ■ Hoogpoort 28 ■ 09
224 37 20 ■ Closed Mon ■ €
Laidback travellers' café adorned
with souvenirs from around the
world. It offers good vegetarian
options, shelves of guidebooks
and two sunny terraces.

7 Karel de Stoute
MAP Q1 ■ Vrouwebroersstraat
2 ■ 09 224 17 35 ■ Closed Sat L, Sun,
Mon ■ €€€
Named after Charles the Bold, Duke
of Burgundy, this is a highly respected
gourmet restaurant in the Patershol
district. Set menus only, permitting
the chefs to excel.

8 Brasserie De Foyer
MAP Q2 ■ Sint-Baafsplein 17
■ 09 234 13 54 ■ Closed Mon, Tue ■ €€
This excellent brasserie is
dramatically located within the
grand 19th-century Koninklijke
Nederlandse Schouwburg (theatre),
with a balcony overlooking Sint-
Baafskathedraal.

9 Frituur Jozef
MAP Q1 ■ Vrijdagmarkt
An old-established chip stand
serving the perfect chips (frites)
and all the trimmings.

10 The House of Eliott
MAP P1 ■ Jan Breydelstraat 36
■ 09 225 21 28 ■ Closed Tue, Wed
■ €€€
Joyously eccentric pseudo-
Edwardian restaurant in a lovely
spot overlooking the canal.

Horse statue, Belga Queen

See map on p108

Streetsmart

Galeries Royales Saint-Hubert, Brussels

Getting To and Around Brussels, Bruges, Antwerp & Ghent

Arriving by Air

Most international flights arrive at Brussels airport, located at Zaventem 14 km (9 miles) northeast of Brussels. **Ryanair** flies to Charleroi (Brussels South), which is 60 km (37 miles) south of the city, as well as to Zaventem.

From Brussels Airport, there are taxi services into town, but the easiest and most economic way to reach central Brussels is by train, with around three trains per hour. There are onward links from Brussels to Bruges, Antwerp and Ghent.

A bus service called Airport Line, run by **STIB/ MIVB**, connects the airport to Brussels' European Quarter. From Charleroi airport, there are shuttle buses to Brussels, and a regular bus service direct to Bruges and Ghent; you can also take the bus to the railway station at Charleroi-Sud, then the train to Brussels, Bruges, Antwerp or Ghent.

Antwerp also has an international airport, with connections to London City Airport, Birmingham, Southampton, and a limited number of other European destinations.

Arriving by Train

The central hub of Belgium's rail network is Brussels, which has three main stations: the Gare du Midi (or Zuidstation), the Gare Centrale (Centraal Station) and the Gare du Nord (Noordstation). **Eurostar** trains from London (as well as international TGV and Thalys trains) arrive at the Gare du Midi. There are good train connections with Bruges, Antwerp and Ghent.

Arriving by Road

To bring a car into Belgium, you must carry a valid EU driving licence, or international driving licence, plus insurance and car-registration documents. You must also carry a warning triangle, first-aid kit and fluorescent safety jacket. You will be driving on the right, so if you are travelling from Britain adjust the angle of your headlamps, or use patches, so that they don't dazzle oncoming drivers. All the motorways in Belgium are toll-free and most are well maintained. Almost all are very well lit at night.

Eurolines and the **Megabus** run regular bus services from London to Brussels, as well as to Bruges, Antwerp and Ghent. There are also services that connect the north of Britain to the Hull-Zeebrugge ferry.

Arriving by Sea

Travellers from Britain can cross the English Channel by ferry, or via the Channel Tunnel. Ferries from Dover land at Calais or Dunkirk (in France), which both lie fairly close to the Belgian border. There is also a service from Hull to Zeebrugge (the port of Bruges) in Belgium. The Channel Tunnel "Shuttle" link, for travellers by car, is operated by **Eurotunnel** and travels between Folkestone and Coquelles (just west of Calais).

Distances Between Cities

Belgium is small – hardly larger than Wales or New Hampshire – and the four cities are all in the north of the country. Brussels is the farthest south; Antwerp lies 55 km (34 miles) due north of Brussels; Ghent lies to the west and about 50 km (31 miles) from Brussels and Antwerp; Bruges lies a further 40 km (25 miles) northwest of Ghent.

Travelling By Train

Belgium's excellent national rail service, **Belgian Rail** (SNCB in French and NMBS in Dutch), is clean, punctual, efficient and reasonably priced. Regular services link all four cities. Its English-language website has timetables, prices and discounts (for children under 12, travellers under 26 or over 65, and for travel at weekends), and you can buy tickets online to print out and carry with you.

Note that if you are travelling by Eurostar, the ticket includes the cost for travelling to other Belgian stations (e.g. Bruges, Antwerp or Ghent), valid for 24 hours after your arrival in Brussels; a return from the destination is likewise valid for 24 hours before your departure back home from Brussels.

By Car

Belgians drive on the right-hand side of the road. There are motorway links between all the cities; the speed limit is 120 kph (75 mph). Breakdown services are offered by the two main Belgian motoring organizations: **Touring** and **VAB**.

There is plenty of parking in and around all the cities; the best plan is to head for one of the main public car parks, which are well signposted. Traffic in city centres, especially Bruges and Ghent, can be bad so visitors are encouraged to use outlying car parks and walk or take the park-and-ride bus. If you are staying overnight, check in advance if your hotel has private parking; this may be relatively expensive, but has the merit of convenience.

Car Rental

All the main car-hire agencies operate in Belgium, and normally have offices at the airports. Usually you get better value if you book a hire car in your home country, linking it with your flight. Note that all the cities are compact; you don't really need a car to get around unless you want to go touring outside the city limits.

By Taxi

Taxis are available at taxi ranks or can be booked by phone. In Brussels, they can occasionally be hailed on the street – but not usually in the other three cities. They cost quite a lot more than public transport. A 10 per cent tip is customary.

By Public Transport

The main transport systems are bus and tram; Brussels also has a Metro (underground railway or subway); Antwerp an underground tram system called the Pre-Metro. Use the buttons on board trams and buses to indicate that you wish to get off at the next stop, and to open the doors. Public transport in Brussels is operated by **STIB** (or **MIVB**); in the other cities the operator is **De Lijn**.

Tickets

Tickets for public transport cover buses, trams and Metro. Single tickets, day passes and preloadable multi-journey MOBIB Basic cards can be bought at ticket booths or stations. Single tickets for buses and trams are also available from the driver. Children under six with a paying adult can travel for free (up to four children per adult). At the start of a journey, validate the ticket or card (in the orange machine or on the red contact pad) on board a bus or tram, or on entering a Metro station; it is then valid for a single journey of up to an hour, including any changes you need to make.

By Bicycle

Belgians are keen cyclists and traffic is usually respectful. You can hire bikes in all the cities. Tourist offices (see p121) will be able to provide details of hire companies.

On Foot

The best way to get around; in all the cities, the main sights are central, and all within easy walking distance. Brussels, Antwerp and Ghent all have extensive pedestrianized zones around the main areas.

DIRECTORY

AIR TRAVEL
Antwerp Airport
w antwerp-airport.be

Brussels Airport
w brusselsairport.be

Charleroi (Brussels South) Airport
w charleroi-airport.com

Ryanair
w ryanair.com

RAIL AND COACH
Belgian Rail
w belgianrail.be

Eurolines
w eurolines.co.uk

Eurostar
w eurostar.com

Eurotunnel
w eurotunnel.com

Megabus
w megabus.com

CAR BREAKDOWN SERVICES
Touring
w touring.be

VAB
w vab.be

PUBLIC TRANSPORT
De Lijn
w delijn.be

STIB/MIVB
w stib.be

Practical Information

Passports and Visas

You need a passport to enter Belgium, valid at least three months beyond the end of your stay. Citizens of the EU, the USA, Australia and New Zealand do not need a visa if staying for less than 90 days. Citizens of other countries should consult their Belgian embassy for information.

Customs Regulations and Immigration

Most goods can be transported between EU countries, including wines, beer, spirits and tobacco, provided they are for your own personal use, and in quantities that reflect this; UK guidelines for maximum quantities are 10 litres of spirits, 800 cigarettes, 90 litres of wine, and 110 litres of beer. Some restrictions apply to meat products, plants and, of course, weapons and narcotics. For non-EU citizens flying into and out of Belgium, national limits apply.

Travel Advice

Visitors can get up-to-date travel information from the Foreign and Commonwealth Office in the UK, the State Department in the USA and the Department of Foreign Affairs and Trade in Australia.

Embassies

Brussels is the "Capital of Europe", so most major countries have embassies in the city – and most of them are located in and around the European Quarter to the east of the centre. Contact your country's embassy if you lose your passport, or in extreme circumstances (for instance, if feel you have been unfairly treated by the police); for the contact details of embassies of the major English-speaking countries, see the Directory box.

Languages

The people of Flanders (which includes Bruges, Antwerp and Ghent) speak Dutch (Nederlands); this may be informally referred to as Flemish *(Vlaams)*, but the official language is categorically Dutch. In Brussels the people speak mostly French or Dutch (some speak the old Bruxellois dialect Marollien).

Generally, English is fairly widely understood, especially by people involved in the tourist trade; in Flanders many people prefer to speak in English rather than French, even though it is one of the Belgian national languages. There is a third official Belgian language, German, but this is spoken primarily in the eastern cantons, on the German border.

Travel Insurance

Take out travel and health insurance when you book your trip. This will allow you to claim compensation if you have to cancel, are delayed or lose your possessions. It should also cover medical costs in case of illness or accident, and – most importantly – the cost of transport to get you home, should you have a major accident or illness.

British citizens can take advantage of reciprocal EU medical agreements, as long as they carry a European Health Insurance Card (EHIC), under which 75 per cent of specified costs can be reclaimed; you usually have to pay for medical treatment in the first instance and reclaim costs later, so be sure to keep all your receipts.

Emergencies

The emergency services are as efficient and reliable as any throughout Europe. For emergency telephone numbers, see the Directory box.

Health

Belgians enjoy a high standard of healthcare; their hospitals – usually located in modern buildings situated in spacious grounds in the suburbs on the periphery of the cities – rank among the best in Europe. This healthcare is extended to foreign visitors, but you will have to pay for it if you are not properly covered by insurance.

Should you suffer an accident or illness, or need emergency dental treatment, ask locally about how best to access these services;

for example, hotels have lists of duty doctors and dentists. Note also that pharmacists are highly trained, and for Belgians are often the first port of call for treatment of minor ailments. But pharmacists know the limits of their jurisdiction, and will refer you to a doctor if necessary. Each commune has a rota of late-night pharmacies.

Personal Security

Belgian cities are not notably dangerous or crime-ridden places, but there is a fair amount of pickpocketing, theft and even car-jacking. If you keep your mental antennae switched on and exercise the same precautions as you would in any other western city, the chances are that you will come through unscathed. One note of caution: Brussels Midi station has a bad reputation for pickpockets and theft: stay alert, particularly in queues and on escalators. If you are the victim of a crime, report it to the police – within 24 hours in the case of theft – if you wish to claim on insurance. Many police officers speak English, and you are likely to get a very professional response.

Identity

Note that you are obliged by law to carry an identity document (for example, a passport or driver's licence) at all times. The police are entitled to ask you to produce this for inspection, but they cannot take it away from you.

Public Holidays

Belgian public holidays are: New Year's Day; Easter Monday; Labour Day (1 May); Ascension Day (6th Thu after Easter); Whit Monday (7th Mon after Easter); Flanders Day (11 July); National (Independence) Day (21 July); Assumption (15 Aug); All Saints' Day (1 Nov); Armistice Day (11 Nov); and Christmas Day. Although banks and post offices will remain closed, some museums and shops may stay open.

Currency and Banking

Belgium's currency is the euro. Notes of other currencies and travellers' cheques can be changed or cashed at a bank or at one of the specialist exchange bureaus. Check the rate of exchange and the commission charged to see whether you are getting a good deal.

Bank and credit cards can be used to draw cash from ATMs (Automatic Teller Machines), which are widespread. Before travelling, check with the bank or card issuer that your card is compatible with Belgian systems (these include Visa, Cirrus, Maestro and Plus), and make sure you know your PIN number. Most major credit and debit cards are accepted in shops, restaurants and hotels.

DIRECTORY

TRAVEL ADVICE

Australian Department of Foreign Affairs and Trade
🆆 dfat.gov.au/travel
🆆 smartraveller.gov.au

UK Foreign and Commonwealth Office
🆆 gov.uk/foreign-travel-advice

US Department of State
🆆 travel.state.gov

EMBASSIES AND CONSULATES

Australian
MAP E4 ■ Avenue des Arts 56, 1000 Brussels (Etterbeek)
🅲 02 286 05 00

British
MAP G4 ■ Avenue d'Auderghem 10, 1040 Brussels (Etterbeek)
🅲 02 287 62 11

Canadian
Avenue de Tervuren 2, 1040 Brussels (Etterbeek)
🅲 02 741 06 11

New Zealand
MAP H5 ■ Avenue des Nerviens 9, 1040 Brussels (Etterbeek)
🅲 02 512 10 40

USA
MAP E3 ■ Boulevard du Régent 27, 1000 Brussels
🅲 02 811 40 00

EMERGENCIES

All services
🅲 112

Ambulance and Fire Services
🅲 100

Police
🅲 101

TELEPHONE CODES

Belgian country code
00 32 (drop the first 0 of the area code)

City area codes
Antwerp: (0)3
Bruges: (0)50
Brussels: (0)2
Ghent: (0)9

Banking Hours

Banks are generally open Mon–Fri 9am–noon and 2–4pm, but some larger branches do not close for lunch. Some banks also open on Saturday mornings. The exchange bureaus have longer opening hours, and may be open through the weekend.

Telephones and Internet

Mobile-phone coverage is good, especially in the cities. Public pay-phones have become virtually redundant as a result – but they still exist, and can be used to make calls abroad; they operate with coins or insertable cards, which can be purchased from newsagents, ticket offices and post offices.

Just about all hotels now offer free Wi-Fi internet facilities for those using their mobile phones or laptops; some also have computer terminals that guests can use in their lobbies. Free or paid-for Wi-Fi access is also available in many bars and cafés.

Post Offices

Post offices are generally open Mon–Fri 9am–5pm. You can buy stamps there and ascertain postage rates for heavier and international items. Main post offices have *poste restante* and banking facilities. Stamps are also available from some tobacconists, newsagents and shops selling postcards. Post boxes are red, often adorned with a post horn and crown, and normally have a label announcing the usual collection times.

Newspapers and TV

The Belgian press is split across the language divide. The main French-language papers are *Le Soir*, *La Libre Belgique* and *La Dernière Heure*; the Dutch-speakers have *Het Laatste Nieuws*, *De Standaard* and *De Morgen*. English-language newspapers are also widely available at newsstands and in bookshops. Brussels also has its own online English-language monthly magazine called *The Bulletin* (www.xpats.com), offering a round-up and analysis of local events, news stories and issues.

As with the newspapers, Belgian television has channels in French and Dutch, and cable brings in a wide choice of channels from all over Europe and the USA. Almost all hotel rooms have televisions.

Time Difference

Belgium is on Central European Time (CET), one hour ahead of Greenwich Mean Time (GMT). It observes Daylight Saving Time, moving the clocks forward in late March and back in late October – so remains one hour ahead of the UK year round, six hours ahead of New York and on the same time as Paris more or less all year round.

Electrical Appliances

Belgium runs on 230 volts AC, using the round two-pin plugs that are common across mainland Europe. The current is fine for the majority of British equipment just to require an adaptor, but American visitors will need a transformer too.

Weather

Belgian weather is typical for northern Europe: a mix of sunshine and rain, distributed across the four seasons. Average seasonal temperatures range from 1°C (34°F) in winter to 19°C (66°F) in summer. All seasons have their merits: summer is most likely to have the best weather, but spring and autumn can be sunny and warm. Winter can be bitterly cold, but the towers and steeples of the city skylines can light up spectacularly in the low-angled sun, and all the cities host Christmas markets to bring seasonal cheer to December.

Regarding clothing and what to pack, assume the worst in weather and you'll be fine. Think in terms of multiple layers, so you can adapt to all weather conditions, and always carry a waterproof one. Be sure to pack stout and comfortable shoes: walking is the best way to see the cities. Bring a compact umbrella that can be easily stored in a backpack or bag.

Disabled Travellers

Historic cities such as Brussels, Bruges, Antwerp and Ghent have developed over centuries with scant attention paid to disabled travellers' needs. Although attitudes are changing, adapting the physical environment to meet their needs will take a long time. Many key sites are in historic areas, where access is hard for people with disabilities. Bruges, especially, will never be able to adapt its narrow pavements and cobbled streets.

Many hotels and B&Bs do not have any special facilities for disabled travellers, and often cannot even contemplate fitting them because of planning restrictions affecting the historic buildings. That said, many hotels, restaurants and tourist attractions are fully adapted, and there is usually no shortage of goodwill to accommodate visitors with special needs: ask in advance, and you should get an honest answer about what is possible and what is likely to prove difficult.

City tourist offices also hold information on facilities for the disabled traveller in hotel rooms, on public transport and taxis, plus wheelchair-accessible toilets, and so on; if this is not published on their website, telephone or email their offices in advance.

Belgian Railways also has useful advice pages on its website.

Tourist Offices

There are Belgian tourist offices in most western capitals, operated by the two main tourist authorities: Tourism Flanders-Brussels (or Visit Flanders); and the Belgian Tourist Office–Brussels & Wallonia (or Wallonia-Brussels Tourism). Each city also has its own tourist office, providing detailed local information and assisting with hotel reservations. All of these tourist offices have useful websites, providing details of key attractions, festivals, events, restaurants and hotels, as well as maps, other useful information and links.

Trips and Tours

Consult the local tourist offices for organized tours of the cities, with guides or audioguides, by bus, walking or cycling, by horse-drawn carriage or by canal (Bruges and Ghent). There are guided tours in an extraordinarily wide range of themes, including Art Nouveau, industrial architecture, Jewish history, folk tales and legends, lace, beer, chocolate, film locations, almshouses, and even death and the macabre.

A number of tour operators organize packaged tours of one or more of the cities, complete with all transport, hotel bookings and catering. Some of these also have a special focus, such as Flemish art and architecture, the battlefields, Belgian beer and/or chocolate.

DIRECTORY

DISABLED TRAVELLERS

Belgium
Access Info
🅦 accessinfo.be

UK
Tourism for All
🅦 tourismforall.org.uk
Youreable.com
🅦 youreable.com

USA
Mobility International
🅦 miusa.org
SATH (Society for Accessible Travel and Hospitality)
🅦 sath.org

TOURIST OFFICES

Antwerp
MAP T1 ■ Grote Markt 13
📞 03 232 01 03
🅦 visitantwerpen.be

Bruges
MAP J5
■ Concertgebouw, 't Zand 34
📞 050 44 46 46
🅦 brugge.be

Brussels
MAP D4 ■ Rue Royale 2
📞 02 513 89 40
🅦 visitbrussels.be

MAP C3 ■ Town Hall, Grand Place
MAP C3 ■ Visit Flanders, Rue du Marché aux Herbes 61
📞 02 504 03 00

Ghent
MAP P1
■ Oude Vismijn, Sint-Veerleplein 5
📞 09 266 56 60
🅦 visitgent.be

TRIPS AND TOURS

ARAU (Architecture/Art Nouveau)
🅦 arau.org

BeerTrips.com
🅦 beertrips.com

Cox & Kings
🅦 coxandkings.co.uk

Flanders Battlefield Tour
🅦 ypres-fbt.com

InTrend Travel (chocolate)
🅦 intrend.com

Martin Randall Travel
🅦 martinrandall.com

Shopping

Belgium can be a rewarding place to shop. The high streets and shopping malls have an excellent range of shops, selling clothes and fashion, chocolates and other food specialities, leatherwork, books and stationery, souvenirs, and so on – generally of excellent quality, and at reasonable prices.

As a general rule, shops are open from 10am to 6pm; small shops such as bakeries and newsagents may open earlier. Some shops close for lunch but stay open later in the evening. On Sundays, larger shops and supermarkets close, but pâtisseries, chocolate shops, delicatessens and tourist shops are likely to remain open. Some shops stay open late on one night of the week.

Note that many goods worth taking home – Trappist beers and other specialist beers, Côte d'Or or Galler chocolates – are found in supermarkets. The larger chains, such as Carrefour and Delhaize chain, tend to be in the suburbs, but they also have mini stores in town.

Where to Eat

The best Belgian restaurants rank among the top in the world, and many of the lesser-known ones are very good indeed. This is partly because the Belgians have a keen instinct for good food, so – as a general rule – look for places where the locals eat. If in doubt, ask for advice at your hotel:

Belgians tend not to give poor advice about food. Above all, avoid tourist-trap restaurants – the ones in the middle of town with plastic-coated menus printed in at least four languages, waiters who solicit your custom at the door and an entirely foreign clientele. These restaurants are unlikely to show why Belgian food is celebrated and cherished by so many.

For the most part restaurants serve classic French cuisine, although Belgium has its own range of robust and tasty dishes, such as *carbonnades flamandes* and *waterzooi (see p61)*.

Good restaurants are busy every day of the week. If you set your heart on going to a particular one, be sure to make a booking – usually easy enough to do over the telephone or Internet; the hotel concierge will be able to help too – and if you change your mind be sure to cancel it.

Look for fixed-price menus (*dagschotel* or *dagmenu* in Dutch; *menu du jour* in French) of two or three courses: these are often the best showcases for the chef's skills and creativity, and can be very good value, especially at lunchtime in top-quality restaurants.

Eating out is often a family event in Belgium; lunch can last half the afternoon. Children get used to this from an early age and may develop surprisingly sophisticated tastes. As a result, children are almost always welcomed in restaurants, and restaurateurs will go

out of their way to satisfy their eating and drinking preferences. Children are also allowed into most cafés and bars.

Vegetarians will notice that Belgium is essentially a carnivorous and fish-loving nation, but most restaurants do provide vegetarian options. There are also some dedicated vegetarian restaurants in all four cities, where chefs apply their characteristic Belgian flare to their dishes. Tourist offices have listings of places to eat.

Value-added tax (TVA/BTW) at 21 per cent and a service charge of 16 per cent can add a lot to a restaurant bill, but both are usually included in the prices quoted in the menu. If you are not sure, don't be afraid to ask. If service is not included, you can add 10 per cent; if it is, you can add a small cash tip, but this at your discretion.

Food and Drink: Good to Know

In certain dishes, beef is served raw. This applies to *Steak Américain*, minced beef – not quite what it might sound like to the uninitiated. Similarly, the Italian dish *carpaccio*, which appears on the menus of many Belgian restaurants, consists of slices of raw beef. Fish is also served raw in the Japanese-influenced fusion dishes, and in salmon or tuna *carpaccio*. Oysters are likewise eaten raw.

Belgian beers are generally somewhat stronger than their

equivalents in Britain and the USA, and range from about 5% to 12% alcohol by volume (sometimes even more). Since beers are generally served in fairly small quantities, the effect can be deceptive – until you stand up. It may need a bit of practice to get the measure of this.

Where to Stay

Belgian hotels are, for the most part, very well run, clean and with a high standard of hospitality based on a sound professional training, a genuine desire to please the customer and the knowledge that there is usually plenty of choice available.

To help you make your selection, there is no shortage of information about accommodation on the internet: most hotels have their own websites, with links for enquiries and bookings – and will often match prices with the booking sites, if you make your reservation directly with them.

You can book by internet or telephone (almost all reception staff speak English). Many hotels require security for a booking, such as a credit card number. If you turn up in a city without a booking, the tourist office (see p121) should be able to help you to find a room.

Hotels prices reflect the predicted ebb and flow of business and holiday trade. Summer is busy in Bruges, but less so in Brussels, Antwerp or the university city of Ghent. Many hotels offer special weekend rates (Fri–Sun and public holidays),

which may be far cheaper than the standard "rack rate". Note that the prices quoted may not always include city or tourism tax, which is usually €2 extra per person per night. Check whether breakfast is included in the rate – it can cost €15 a head or more per person, if you pay for the hotel breakfast separately. Many hotels pride themselves on their breakfasts, offering a generous buffet featuring cereals, croissants, cold meats and cheeses, fruit, yogurts and juices, and sometimes bacon and eggs – so if this is included in the price of the room, it makes a significant difference to their value for money.

The official star system for rating hotels in Belgium is based more on facilities than on things that really make a difference, such as decor, tranquillity and quality of service. Two-star hotels may actually be more rewarding and agreeable than five-star ones.

In increasing numbers, private citizens in the cities are opening their homes for bed-and-breakfast accommodation, and some of these are in delightful historic houses, right in the centre. They can be good value for money – often around €55–€95 for a double room, per night, although the most luxurious are considerably more expensive – and the best tend to be booked up months in advance. You can find many of these properties on the internet.

Youth hostels offer by far the cheapest

accommodation in Belgium – as little as €20 per person, including breakfast. Most offer a mixture of two-, three-, four- and six-bedroom dormitories with shared washing facilities, but there is an increasing trend for upmarket hostels that offer en suites. Hostels also have lively bars, kitchens for preparing your own meals, and internet facilities – all good for meeting other travellers.

A cheap option for families and groups, at under €20 per family per night, is to stay at one of Belgium's efficiently run camping and caravanning sites. Needless to say, they are not near the city centres. Tourist offices will have details.

DIRECTORY

BED-AND-BREAKFASTS

Bed & Breakfast Antwerpen
W gastenkamers antwerpen.be

Bed & Brussels
W bnb-brussels.be

Corporation of Bruges B&B
W brugge-bedand breakfast.com

Guild of Guesthouses in Ghent
W bedandbreakfast-gent.be

BOOKING SITES

W booking.com
W expedia.com
W galahotels.com
W lastminute.com
W tripadvisor.com
W laterooms.com

Places to Stay

PRICE CATEGORIES
For a standard double room per night (with breakfast if included), including taxes and extra charges.

€ under 100   €€ €100–250   €€€ over €250

Brussels Hotels: Top of the Range

Brussels Marriott Hotel Grand Place
MAP B2 ■ Rue Auguste Orts 3–7, 1000 BRU ■ 02 516 90 90 ■ www.marriott.com ■ €€
A Marriott with unique character, located near the Bourse and the Grand Place. Ideal for business, shopping and leisure.

The Dominican
MAP C2 ■ Rue Léopold 9, 1000 BRU ■ 02 203 08 08 ■ www.thedominican.be ■ €€
This luxurious hotel on a quiet street cannot be beaten for location, right behind Théâtre Royal de la Monnaie and within walking distance of the Grand Place. Award-winning architects have created a pleasant private courtyard over which the rooms look, and a sumptuous Grand Lounge.

The Hotel
MAP C5 ■ Boulevard de Waterloo 38, 1000 BRU ■ 02 504 11 11 ■ www.thehotel-brussels.be ■ €€
This high-rise may not look much from the outside, but the inside is brimming with surprises, including contemporary decor and stunning views from the higher rooms, as well as the 23rd-floor sauna and gym. Excellent service.

Hotel Métropole
MAP C2 ■ Place de Brouckère 31, 1000 BRU ■ 02 217 23 00 ■ www.metropolehotel.com ■ €€
A landmark Brussels hotel with lavish *belle époque* reception and bar. The large, elegant rooms are fresh and decorated in pretty colours. There is a fully equipped fitness centre. Centrally located, not far from Place Ste-Catherine and Place St-Géry.

Manos Premier
MAP C6 ■ Chaussée de Charleroi 100–106, 1060 BRU ■ 02 537 96 82 ■ www.manospremier.com ■ €€
This privately owned five-star boutique hotel offers 50 rooms styled with period furniture, an on-site spa and a restaurant. The reception has an old Parisian-style feel with marble and gilt-edged mirrors. Guests can also enjoy the peaceful private garden. Very calm yet close to the bustling Avenue Louise.

Royal Windsor
MAP C3 ■ Rue Duquesnoy 5, 1000 BRU ■ 02 505 55 55 ■ www.royalwindsorbrussels.com ■ €€
Equidistant from the Grand Place and the Musées Royaux des Beaux-Arts, this elegant and sumptuous hotel is part of the Warwick group. It has a restaurant, bar and fitness suite.

Sofitel Brussels Le Louise
MAP C6 ■ Avenue de la Toison d'Or 40, 1050 BRU ■ 02 514 22 00 ■ www.accorhotels.com ■ €€
Don't be deterred by the fact that this is a chain hotel, Sofitel brought in revered designer Antoine Pinto to redefine this five-star hotel with a glamorous, eclectic vibe. Rooms are plush, and the restaurant has a lovely sunny terrace.

Amigo
MAP B3 ■ Rue de l'Amigo 1–3, 1000 BRU ■ 02 547 47 47 ■ www.hotelamigo.com ■ €€€
Steps away from the Grand Place, this smart hotel occupies the site of a 16th-century prison. Rooms are decked out in rich Flemish fabrics, and Magritte prints grace the bathroom walls.

Astoria
MAP D2 ■ Rue Royale 103, 1000 BRU ■ 02 227 05 05 ■ €€€
With its palatial lobby and spectacular public rooms, the Astoria looks as if it dates from the 18th century, but was actually built in 1909. It is located in the Upper Town, near to the Royal Palace. Both Churchill and Eisenhower stayed here. The Astoria is closed for renovation, so call ahead.

Radisson Blu Royal

MAP C2 ■ Rue Fossé-aux-Loups 47, 1000 BRU ■ 02 219 28 28 ■ www.radissonblu.com ■ €€€
The foyer, showcasing the work of renowned Belgian architect Michel Jaspers, is breathtaking – a towering atrium, with tropical plants and fountains filling its base, and glass-fronted lifts rising into the firmament. The hotel has a renowned restaurant, the Sea Grill (see p80).

Brussels: Hotels of Character

Espérance

MAP C1 ■ Rue du Finistère 1–3, 1000 BRU ■ 02 219 10 28 ■ www.hotel-esperance.be ■ €
This 1930s Art Deco gem is hidden away near Place des Martyrs (see p76). Most rooms are modern, but Room 7 still retains its old splendour. The tavern/breakfast room has hardly changed and is a must for evening drinks.

Hotel Bloom!

MAP E1 ■ Rue Royale 250, 1210 BRU ■ 02 220 69 05 ■ www.hotelbloom.com ■ €
A bright, fresh, modern hotel; all-white rooms each with a fresco painted by a young European artist. Behind the botanical gardens with easy access to the Gare du Nord and the city centre.

Meininger

MAP A2 ■ Quai Hainaut 33, 1080 BRU ■ 02 588 14 74 ■ www.meininger-hotels.com ■ €
Housed in a former brewery, this backpacker-style, carbon-neutral,

three-star hotel has over 170 fun rooms. Family rooms are available too.

Vintage Hotel

MAP C6 ■ Rue Dejoncker 45, 1060 BRU ■ 02 533 99 80 ■ www.vintagehotel.be ■ €
A 1960s-styled boutique hotel close to fashionable Avenue Louise. Rooms feature bubble lamps and psychedelic wallpaper. At night, the breakfast room turns into a wine bar.

Le Dixseptième

MAP C3 ■ Rue de la Madeleine 25, 1000 BRU ■ 02 517 17 17 ■ www.ledixseptieme.be ■ €€
There is no other place quite like this in Brussels: an utterly charming and fascinating small hotel in the late-17th-century residence of the Spanish ambassador. It has a number of suites – named after Belgian artists – ingeniously set beneath the roof beams, and furnished with a mixture of antique charm and modern flair.

Ibis Styles Brussels Louise

MAP C6 ■ Avenue Louise 212, 1050 BRU ■ 02 644 29 29 ■ www.ibis.com ■ €€
Once independently run, the former White Hotel is now part of the Ibis chain, but it retains its contemporary all-white theme and continues to showcase artwork of young Belgian designers.

Pantone Hotel

MAP C6 ■ Place Loix 1, 1060 BRU ■ 02 541 48 98 ■ www.pantonehotel.com ■ €€
The world's first hotel to apply the standardized

Pantone colour-matching system used by designers from every continent. White walls and bedding allow colourful accessories to shine. Some rooms have rooftop views of the Lower Town.

Le Plaza

MAP C1 ■ Boulevard Adolphe Max 118–26, 1000 BRU ■ 02 278 01 00 ■ www.leplaza-brussels.be ■ €€
You feel a bit like a guest of Louis XVI in the palatial foyer and public rooms of this grand hotel, with its stucco, gilt, and lavish ceiling paintings. The guest rooms maintain the same high standard of spacious comfort.

Warwick Barsey Hotel

Avenue Louise 381–3, 1050 BRU ■ 02 649 98 00 ■ www.warwickbarsey.com ■ €€
Located at the southern end of stylish Avenue Louise, this hotel was decorated by French designer Jacques Garcia in an opulent Edwardian style. The rooms exude a sense of luxurious, silky comfort. The private terrace is a bonus in summer.

Odette en Ville

MAP D8 ■ Rue de Châtelain 25, 1050 BRU ■ 02 640 26 26 ■ www.chez-odette.com ■ €€€
An intimate eight-room boutique hotel located in a 1920s building. Rooms are decorated with calming greys and whites, and feature first-rate fixtures such as under-floor heating. Romantic restaurant with freshly cut roses and open fire.

Brussels Hotels: Business and Budget

2GO4 Grand Place
MAP C3 ▪ Rue de Haringstraat 6–8, 1000 BRU ▪ 02 219 30 19 ▪ www.2go4.be ▪ €
Just off the Grand Place, this is Brussels' only city-centre hostel. With options to suit all budgets, the range of rooms on offer includes multi-share rooms, singles and doubles, with or without private bathrooms. There are excellent kitchen facilities and free internet access.

Aloft Brussels Schuman
MAP G4 ▪ Place Jean Rey, 1040 BRU ▪ 02 800 08 88 ▪ www.aloftbrussels.com ▪ €
Funky, affordable boutique-design hotel in the heart of the EU district. Instead of a restaurant, there is a 24-hour "food station" serving snacks, sandwiches, salads and treats, as well as drinks. A choice of breakfast options is also available. Other facilities include free Wi-Fi, a fitness centre and a lively bar with live music.

Aqua Hotel
MAP D5 ▪ Rue de Stassart 43, 1050 BRU ▪ 02 213 01 01 ▪ www.aqua-hotel-brussels.com ▪ €€
Crisp, clean, good-value hotel that is popular with businesspeople looking for something a bit different – a huge, blue Arne Quinze sculpture twists through the entire building. In a quiet street close to the Metro.

Marivaux
MAP C1 ▪ Boulevard Adolphe Max 98, 1000 BRU ▪ 02 227 03 00 ▪ www.hotelmarivaux.be ▪ €€
A simple but satisfactory business hotel with contemporary-styled guest rooms and state-of-the-art meeting rooms. Relax in the cocktail bar or enjoy a fusion-cuisine meal in the elegant brasserie.

The Progress Hotel
MAP G1 ▪ Rue du Progrès 9, 1210 BRU ▪ 02 205 17 00 ▪ www.progresshotel.be ▪ €€
Friendly, small hotel close to the Botanical Gardens with functional black-and-white rooms. After a day of business meetings, guests can relax on massage chairs in the covered winter garden with its 100-year-old olive trees. Airport pickups and customized tours can be arranged through the concierge.

Radisson Red Brussels
MAP E5 ▪ Rue d'Idalie 35, 1050 BRU ▪ 02 626 81 11 ▪ www.radissonred.com ▪ €€
A deluxe hotel adjacent to the European Parliament, with spacious designer bedrooms, premier meeting rooms, sauna, fitness centre and Willards bar/restaurant.

Scandic Grand Place
MAP C3 ▪ Rue d'Arenberg 18, 1000 BRU ▪ 02 548 18 11 ▪ www.scandichotels.com ▪ €€
It's not quite on the Grand Place, but near enough to make this straightforward, professional hotel an attractive proposition:

it offers very competitive prices, if your timing is right. The decor is both stylish and functional, as the brand's name would suggest. There is also a sauna and a fitness centre.

Thon Hotel EU
MAP F4 ▪ Rue de la Loi 75, 1040 BRU ▪ 02 204 39 11 ▪ www.thonhotels.com ▪ €€
This multi-coloured hotel offers functional, modern rooms, free Wi-Fi, conference rooms, a fitness centre, a restaurant, and even a small shopping mall.

Silken Berlaymont
MAP G3 ▪ Boulevard Charlemagne 11–19, 1000 BRU ▪ 02 231 09 09 ▪ www.hoteles-silken.com ▪ €€€
Close to the heart of European government, this eco-friendly hotel is favoured by diplomats, politicians and journalists. They make full use of its state-of-the-art communication systems, fitness centre, Turkish baths and sauna.

Sofitel Brussels Europe
MAP G5 ▪ Place Jourdan 1, 1040 BRU ▪ 02 235 51 00 ▪ www.accorhotels.com ▪ €€€
Elegant five-star hotel just a stone's throw from the European Parliament. The spacious rooms are beautifully designed in contemporary style, and feature luxury bathrooms that come with designer toiletries. Extras include 11 meeting rooms, a hammam, a fitness centre, a rooftop terrace and an on-site chocolate shop for last-minute gifts.

Bruges Hotels: Luxury

De Castillion
MAP K4 ▪ Heilige Geeststraat 1 ▪ 050 34 30 01 ▪ www.castillion.be ▪ €€

Occupying a 17th-century bishop's residence in the west of the city, this comfortable hotel has imaginatively decorated bedrooms and bathrooms. The high standard of the rooms is matched by its remarkable Art Deco lounge and bar.

Hotel de Orangerie
MAP K4 ▪ Kartuizerinnenstraat 10 ▪ 050 34 16 49 ▪ www.hotelorangerie.be ▪ €€

This delightful hotel in a 15th-century convent has a gorgeous panelled breakfast room and lounge with a terrace overlooking the canal. The hotel exudes character and charm.

NH Brugge
MAP J5 ▪ Boeveriestraat 2 ▪ 050 44 97 11 ▪ www.nh-hotels.com ▪ €€

Once a 17th-century monastery, this building retains some lovely features, such as stained-glass windows, large fireplaces and wooden beams. The rooms are in a modern style, but the Jan Breydel bar has old-world charm.

Die Swaene
MAP L4 ▪ Steenhouwersdijk 1 ▪ 050 34 27 98 ▪ www.dieswaene.be ▪ €€

An opulent, romantic hotel with rooms in the 18th-century building and in the modern "pergola" looking out over the pretty canal. Amenities include a glamorous lounge in an old guildhall, an indoor swimming pool and a gastronomic restaurant.

Bonifacius
MAP K5 ▪ Groeninge 4 ▪ 050 49 00 49 ▪ www.bonifacius.be ▪ €€€

A superb boutique B&B in a 16th-century building overlooking the canal and Bonifacius Bridge. Each room is decorated with rich fabrics and antiques, and features an en-suite granite bathroom with Jacuzzi bath. Bonifacius is located opposite the Michelin-starred Den Gouden Harynck restaurant (see p98).

Crowne Plaza Hotel
MAP L4 ▪ Burg 10 ▪ 050 44 68 44 ▪ www.ihg.com ▪ €€€

You could not get more central if you tried: the Crowne Plaza overlooks the Burg at the very heart of Bruges. A modern establishment, it also incorporates some historic remains: the excavated foundations of the medieval church of St Donatian. The hotel has an indoor swimming pool, the PlazaCafé and its own car park.

Heritage
MAP K3 ▪ Niklaas Desparsstraat 11 ▪ 050 44 44 44 ▪ www.hotel-heritage.com ▪ €€€

Located in a 19th-century mansion, in the old merchant quarter to the north of the Markt, this hotel boasts the respected restaurant, Le Mystique, plus a spa and a fitness room in its 14th-century cellar, and a sun deck with city views on the roof.

Hotel Aragon
MAP K3 ▪ Naaldenstraat 22 ▪ 050 33 35 33 ▪ www.hotelaragon.be ▪ €€€

A well-presented, well-managed hotel close to the centre. It's part of the Swan Hotel Collection, which includes the Dukes' Palace. The hotel also has eight apartments nearby, which can sleep up to seven people.

Hotel Dukes' Palace
MAP K4 ▪ Prinsenhof 8 ▪ 050 44 78 88 ▪ www.hoteldukespalace.com ▪ €€€

This former ducal palace has definitely earned its five stars thanks to the spa pool, art gallery and chapel. The Manuscript restaurant serves a great breakfast. The bar is not cheap, but locals seem to think it's worth it.

The Pand Hotel
MAP L4 ▪ Pandreitje 16 ▪ 050 34 06 66 ▪ www.pandhotel.com ▪ €€€

This boutique hotel, in a fine 18th-century town house, is the ideal place for a romantic getaway. Close to the Burg in a pretty tree-lined street, it is beautifully decorated in a deeply upholstered style, with canopied beds.

De Tuilerieën
MAP L4 ▪ Dijver 7 ▪ 050 34 36 91 ▪ www.hotel tuilerieen.com ▪ €€€

In a 15th-century nobleman's house overlooking the canal, this lavish hotel has hosted many a celebrity. Chocolate fountain in the breakfast bar plus swimming pool, steam room and bar.

For a key to hotel price categories see p124

Bruges Hotels: Mid-range

Adornes
MAP L3 ▪ Sint-Annarei 26 ▪ 050 34 13 36 ▪ www. adornes.be ▪ Closed Jan ▪ €€

The Adornes is located in a renovated set of 16th- to 18th-century mansions overlooking the canal in the quieter, eastern part of the city, yet within walking distance of the centre. The decor, with its exposed beams, has rustic charm. Guests have free use of bicycles. Small pets are allowed.

Egmond
MAP K6 ▪ Minnewater 15 ▪ 050 34 14 45 ▪ www.egmond.be ▪ €€
The Egmond is located in an 18th-century country house a short walk from the centre of Bruges. With its own little tree-shaded park and classic interiors, it feels like a world apart.

Hotel Jacobs
MAP L2 ▪ Baliestraat 1 ▪ 050 33 98 31 ▪ www. hoteljacobs.com ▪ €€
This good-value hotel is in the peaceful Sint-Gillis neighbourhood. Housed in a traditional step-gabled building, it offers clean, comfortable public areas and cosy bedrooms with free Wi-Fi. Close to the main shops, restaurants and museums.

Hotel Malleberg
MAP L4 ▪ Hoogstraat 7 ▪ 050 34 41 11 ▪ www. malleberg.be ▪ €€
This home-from-home tastefully decorated hotel located in a town house is family-run and close to the Markt. The hearty buffet breakfast is served in a vaulted-ceiling basement. There is free Wi-Fi available in both the guest rooms and common areas. Room rates inclusive of tickets to various attractions can be arranged.

Jan Brito
MAP L4 ▪ Freren Fonteinstraat 1 ▪ 050 33 06 01 ▪ www.janbrito.com ▪ €€
Centrally located, between the Burg and the Koningin Astridpark, the Jan Brito occupies an attractive 16th-century building with a step-gabled, brick façade. The charming public rooms are decorated in Louis XVI style. There is also a pretty garden.

De' Medici
MAP L2 ▪ Potterierei 15 ▪ 050 33 98 33 ▪ www. hoteldemedici.com ▪ €€
This smart, modern hotel, overlooking the canal, is a member of the Golden Tulip group. It has a health centre with a gym, sauna and steam room, and a bar that looks over a lovely Japanese-inspired garden.

Navarra
MAP K3 ▪ Sint-Jakobsstraat 41 ▪ 050 34 05 61 ▪ www. hotelnavarra.com ▪ €€
The former trading house of the merchants of Navarre is now a hotel of unusual elegance sited to the north of the Markt. Navarra offers a high standard of service and comfort, including a fitness centre, swimming pool and jazz bar.

Oud Huis de Peellaert
MAP L4 ▪ Hoogstraat 20 ▪ 050 33 78 89 ▪ www. depeellaert.be ▪ €€
Chandeliers, antique furniture and a beautiful spiral staircase set the tone in this pair of grand 19th-century mansions, elegantly and sympathetically restored. High standards of comfort and service prevail, with a gym and sauna in the 16th-century cellars, making this a special place to stay in the heart of historic Bruges.

Park Hotel
MAP J5 ▪ Vrijdagmarkt 5 ▪ 050 33 33 64 ▪ www. parkhotel-brugge.be ▪ €€
The Park Hotel is well run, with a charming plant-filled breakfast/lunch room and functional guest rooms. It overlooks the Zand, the spacious market square to the west of the city, and is only 10 minutes' walk from the city centre. There is a spacious car park under the hotel.

Prinsenhof
MAP K4 ▪ Ontvangersstraat 9 ▪ 050 34 26 90 ▪ www. prinsenhof.be ▪ €€
This regular award-winner is tucked away down a side street in the west of the city, in an area once occupied by the splendid palace of the dukes of Burgundy. Something of the dukes' grand style pervades the decor – on a smaller scale, of course. All of the comfortable guest rooms

are individually decorated. A hearty and varied buffet breakfast is included.

Bruges Hotels: Budget

Bauhaus Hotel

MAP M3 ■ Langestraat 135 (reception at 145) ■ 050 34 10 93 ■ www.bauhaus.be ■ €
A popular, energetic and friendly hostel. Located in the east of the city, a 15-minute walk from the centre, it prides itself on its cheap accommodation. The Bauhaus bar serves more than 25 Belgian beers, and bar snacks. Free Wi-Fi.

Charlie Rockets

MAP L4 ■ Hoogstraat 19 ■ 050 33 06 60 ■ www.charlierockets.com ■ €
Located just a two-minute walk from the Burg is this party hostel, above an American-style bar with pool tables and live music on Friday nights. Free internet access. With no curfew in place, don't expect peace and quiet.

Hostel de Passage

MAP K4 ■ Dweerstraat 26 ■ 050 34 02 32 ■ www.passagebruges.com ■ €
An interesting budget hotel with just 10 simple, well-presented rooms (six doubles, two triples and two quadruples; prices quoted are per person). It is attached to the equally alluring Gran Kaffee de Passage (see p99).

Hotel Canalview Ter Reien

MAP L3 ■ Langestraat 1 ■ 050 34 91 00 ■ www.hotelterreien.be ■ €
Fetchingly perched beside the canal a little to the east of the Burg. Ter Reien's rooms are clean, and the double bedrooms have capsule bathrooms. A room with a courtyard view is also good. Guests need to pay to access Wi-Fi.

Hotel Ter Brughe

MAP K3 ■ Oost Gistelhof 2 ■ 050 34 03 24 ■ www.hotelterbrughe.com ■ €
Hotel Ter Brughe is located just north of the Augustijnenrei canal in a charming web of old streets. This well-run hotel occupies a listed 16th-century house overlooking the canal, which boasts some impressive ancient wooden beams, especially in the breakfast room and in some of the spacious guest rooms.

Lucca

MAP K3 ■ Naaldenstraat 30 ■ 050 34 20 67 ■ www.hotellucca.be ■ €
The 18th-century Neo-Classical exterior conceals an even older interior, with a vaulted medieval cellar in which guests breakfast. This was once the lodge of the merchants of Lucca – with connec-tions to Giovanni Arnolfini, the banker who features in Jan van Eyck's famous painting, *The Arnolfini Portrait*. The rooms are quaintly old-fashioned – a fact reflected in the attractive room price.

De Pauw

MAP L2 ■ Sint-Gilliskerkhof 8 ■ 050 33 71 18 ■ www.hoteldepauw.be ■ €
This pretty, family-run hotel, with its weathered brick exterior draped with flowers, is located close to the old parish church of Sint-Gillis, in the quiet and historic northern part of town – but still just a 10-minute walk from the centre. The interior is styled like a private home, with a welcome to match.

Hotel Biskajer

MAP K3 ■ Biskajersplein 4 ■ 050 34 15 06 ■ www.hotelbiskajer.com ■ €€
This small 17-room hotel just north of the Markt may lack amenities, but this makes it an affordable option. All rooms have en-suite bathrooms, and a buffet breakfast is included in the price. There is a smart breakfast room and a small, cosy bar stocked with local beers. No children under 16.

Patritius

MAP L3 ■ Riddersstraat 11 ■ 050 33 84 54 ■ www.hotelpatritius.be ■ €€
Given its reasonable prices, the family-owned Patritius occupies a surprisingly grand 19th-century mansion located to the north-east of the Markt. The stylish rooms and interior garden are bonuses too.

Ter Duinen

MAP L2 ■ Langerei 52 ■ 050 33 04 37 ■ www.terduinenhotel.eu ■ €€
This charming small hotel may seem a little out of the way in the north of the city, but the centre of Bruges is only a 15-minute walk away. Well-presented rooms (some with canal views) are double-glazed and air-conditioned, and the public rooms are stylish.

Antwerp Hotels

Pulcinella
MAP T2 ■ Bogaardeplein 1 ■ 03 234 03 14 ■ www.jeugdherbergen.be ■ €
This is possibly the smartest youth hostel in Belgium, featuring a minimalist interior with a mix of two-, four- and six-bed rooms. There's also a bar. Accessible to disabled travellers, and no curfew.

Firean
Karel Oomsstraat 6 ■ 03 237 02 60 ■ www.hotelfirean.com ■ €€
A highly respected family-run hotel in a 1920s Art Deco mansion. Although located further out of the centre than other options, Firean's charm makes the journey worthwhile. Rooms are spacious and feature rich fabrics.

Hotel Docklands
Kempisch Dok Westkaai 84–90 ■ 03 231 07 26 ■ www.hotel docklands.be ■ €€
Located in the up-and-coming docklands a 15-minute walk north of the centre, this Best Western-owned hotel sports a black-and-white colour scheme in the rooms and public areas. There is a well-stocked breakfast buffet and plenty of dining options nearby.

Hotel Rubens
MAP T1 ■ Oude Beurs 29 ■ 03 222 48 48 ■ www.hotelrubensantwerp.be ■ €€
A quiet, romantic option located just behind the Grote Markt. Spacious one-bedroom suites have separate living rooms and lovely views. There is a pretty terrace, where breakfast can be taken in warm weather.

Julien
MAP T1 ■ Korte Nieuwstraat 24 ■ 03 229 06 00 ■ www.hotel-julien.com ■ €€
Fashioned out of two town houses linked by a green patio, this contemporary hotel has stylish interiors. Ideally located between the Meir shopping area and the cathedral.

Leopold
MAP V3 ■ Quinten Matsijslei 25 ■ 03 231 15 15 ■ www.leopold hotelantwerp.com ■ €€
This unassuming modern hotel is part of the small Leopold group. The hotel is well run, agreeably comfortable and con-veniently located within easy walking distance of Centraal station, the Rubenshuis and the Meir shopping street. It has its own bar and a gym, and just across the street is the pretty Stadspark.

Matelote
MAP T2 ■ Haarstraat 11A ■ 03 201 88 00 ■ www.hotel-matelote.be ■ €€
This converted town house near the River Scheldt offers nine dazzlingly light rooms, all with minimalist decor and modern facil-ities. Prices include free Wi-Fi and mineral water; a buffet breakfast is avail-able at an additional cost.

Mercure Antwerpen Centrum Opera
MAP U2 ■ Molenbergstraat 9–11 ■ 03 232 76 75 ■ www.accorhotels.com ■ €€
Located just behind the Meir shopping street, this chain hotel is fresh, modern and efficient. Rooms are spacious and comfortable. There is a delicious breakfast buffet and a cosy bar with a good choice of wines.

Radisson Blu Astrid Hotel
MAP V2 ■ Koningin Astridplein 7 ■ 03 203 12 34 ■ www.radissonblu.com ■ €€
This is a large and well-run hotel, close to Centraal station, east of the city centre. It offers extensive conference facilities, and is well suited to: the business traveller. There's also a fitness suite and swimming pool.

't Sandt
MAP T2 ■ Zand 17 ■ 03 232 93 90 ■ www.hotel-sandt.be ■ €€
This hotel in an old patrician mansion, just to the west of the cathedral, and close to the river, has been elegantly kitted out in a style you might call "Neo-Rococo". All the suites, including the luxurious penthouse, are set around a courtyard garden.

Theater Hotel
MAP U2 ■ Arenbergstraat 30 ■ 03 203 54 10 ■ www.vhv-hotels.be ■ €€
In the theatre district of Antwerp, this modern hotel lies in a convenient location close to the Rubenshuis, and is a short walk from the cathedral via some of Antwerp's best shopping streets. The rooms are decorated in a neat minimalist style.

Ghent Hotels

Hostel 47
MAP R1 ■ Blekerijstraat 47 ■ 0478 71 28 27 ■ www.hostel47.com ■ €
This high-spec, privately owned youth hostel offers nine rooms within walking distance of Ghent's historical centre. It has trendy common areas with free Wi-Fi and there is no curfew for guests. The rooms sleep 2–6 people; prices include breakfast.

Monasterium PoortAckere
MAP P2 ■ Oude Houtlei 58 ■ 09 269 22 10 ■ www.monasterium.be ■ €
Here is an interesting experience: a hotel in a converted convent. An air of tranquillity pervades the (largely 19th-century) buildings and grounds. A special place, enhanced by a warm welcome and a relaxed atmosphere – and a convenient location just west of the city centre.

Erasmus Hotel
MAP P2 ■ Poel 25 ■ 09 224 21 95 ■ www.erasmushotel.be ■ €€
This 16th-century patrician's house, west of the city centre, retains many of its original features and is decorated with antiques. Its old-fashioned charm creates the perfect backdrop for visiting the historic city.

Ghent River Hotel
MAP Q1 ■ Waaistraat 5 ■ 09 266 10 10 ■ www.ghent-river-hotel.be ■ €€
This functional, modern hotel has 77 rooms occupying a converted 16th-century house and a 19th-century factory. It is located on the bank of the River Leie close to the lively Vrijdagmarkt. The breakfast room boasts stunning views of the city.

Hotel de Flandre
MAP P2 ■ Poel 1–2 ■ 09 266 06 00 ■ www.hoteldeflandre.be ■ €€
Tucked behind the Korenlei quayside, this stylish town house has retained plenty of period detail in its public areas while its bedrooms are calm and comfortable.

Hotel Gravensteen
MAP P1 ■ Jan Breydelstraat 35 ■ 09 225 11 50 ■ www.gravensteen.be ■ €€
Sitting opposite the Castle of the Counts, this 49-room hotel has a wow-factor entrance, comfortable rooms, a cosy bar with a great selection of Belgian beers, sauna and fitness room. The breakfast buffet offers a great selection of hot and cold choices. Guests have access to a private car park and are permitted to bring small pets.

Hotel Harmony
MAP Q1 ■ Kraanlei 37 ■ 09 324 26 80 ■ www.hotel-harmony.be ■ €€
A stylish, family-run hotel located in Patershol, the oldest quarter of Ghent. The hotel features a courtyard swimming pool and a series of upscale rooms facing the canal; all have roof terraces with views over the city.

Hotel Onderbergen
MAP P3 ■ Onderbergen 69 ■ 09 223 62 00 ■ www.hotelonderbergen.be ■ €€
Just 3 minutes' walk from Sint-Baafskathedraal, this boutique hotel is decorated in a cool, pared-down style, Hotel Onderbergen occupies a historic house, where some of the spacious rooms have exposed beams, and also offers family rooms for up to six people, and an apartment.

Ibis Gent Centrum Kathedraal
MAP Q2 ■ Limburgstraat 2 ■ 09 233 00 00 ■ www.accorhotels.com ■ €€
Right in the centre of Ghent, overlooking Sint-Baafskathedraal, this is a well-run, modern and attractive member of the reliable Ibis chain. There are plenty of eateries to choose from nearby. The private paying car park has limited spaces.

NH Gent Belfort
MAP Q2 ■ Hoogpoort 63 ■ 09 233 33 31 ■ www.nh-hotels.com ■ €€
This chain certainly knows how to deliver style and comfort. The Belfort has all the facilities of a hotel of this rank, including a fitness room and sauna, and is very centrally located, opposite the Stadhuis.

Sandton Grand Hotel Reylof
MAP P2 ■ Hoogstraat 36 ■ 09 235 40 70 ■ www.sandton.eu ■ €€€
A grand 18th-century mansion and a modern extension provide luxury accommodation close to the historic centre. There is a courtyard garden, bar, highly regarded restaurant, and a "wellness centre".

For a key to hotel price categories see p124

Index

Acknowledgments

Author

Antony Mason is the author of a number of guide books, including the Cadogan City Guides to *Bruges* and to *Brussels (with Bruges, Ghent and Antwerp)*, and the main contributor to the *DK Eyewitness Guide to Belgium and Luxembourg*. He writes frequently for the *Daily Telegraph* on Brussels and Belgium and is the author of the volume on *The Belgians* in the humorous Xenophobe's Guides series – along with more than 80 other books on history, geography, exploration and art. He lives in London with his Belgian wife Myriam.

Publishing Director Georgina Dee

Publisher Vivien Antwi

Design Director Phil Ormerod

Editorial Michelle Crane, Hayley Maher, Freddie Marriage, Scarlett O'Hara, Aakanksha Singh, Jackie Staddon, Hollie Teague

Design Richard Czapnik, Marisa Renzullo, Richa Verma

Commissioned Photography Demetrio Carrasco, Rough Guides/Jean-Christophe Godet

Picture Research Susie Peachey, Ellen Root, Lucy Sienkowska, Oran Tarjan

Cartography Dominic Beddow, Simonetta Giori, Zafar-ul Islam Khan, Suresh Kumar, Casper Morris

DTP Jason Little, George Nimmo

Production Niamh Tierney

Factchecker Dan Colwell

Proofreader Clare Peel

Indexer Hilary Bird

Illustrator chrisorr.com

First edition created by DP Services, a division of Duncan Petersen Publishing Ltd

Picture Credits

The publisher would like to thank the following for their kind permission to reproduce their photographs:

Key: a-above; b-below/bottom; c-centre; f-far; l-left; r-right; t-top

123RF.com: Nattee Chalermtiragool 14cla; Botond Horváth 12tr;

4Corners: Richard Taylor 4crb.

akg-images: Erich Lessing 17br.

Alamy Stock Photo: Alko 60ca; Alpineguide 51tl; Arterra Picture Library/De Meester Johan 61cla, 66br; © www.atomium.be SABAM Belgium 2016 /Prisma Bildagentur AG/Raga Jose Fuste 83tl' Stephen Barrie 62t; Bildagentur-online/ McPhoto-Weber 54crb; Peter Cavanagh 58tl; Clement Philippe/Arterra Picture Library 93cl; Gary Cook 28br, 95b; dpa picture alliance 63tr;

Sergey Dzyuba 68b; Eye Ubiquitous/Bernard Regent 12bl; © Hergé-Moulinsart /Neil Farrin 12br; Kevin Galvin 96br; Garden Photo World/ David C Phillips 74cl, 77cl; Garden Photo World/ David C. Phillips 51crb; Kevin George 55tl, 76b; Hemis / Ludovic Maisant 48tl, 106bl, 106br; Maurizio Borgese 23cl; © Hergé-Moulinsart / Jochen Tack 56bc; © Hergé-Moulinsart /Maurice Savage 63clb; Heritage Image Partnership Ltd/ Fine Art Images 41crb; New Horizons 15cla; Peter Horree 58cb, 112clb; imageBROKER/KFS 35cl; Eric James 15bc; Oliver Knight 48br, 78cla, 113bl; Douglas Lander 7cr; Peter Lane 96cla; Maurice Savage 12c; Bombaert Patrick 53tr; Pictorial Press 59tr; PjrTravel 14bl, 16bl, 46br; Prisma Bildagentur AG/Raga Jose Fuste 68tl; Juergen Ritterbach 86cl; sagaphoto.com/ Stephane Gautier 80br; Neil Setchfield 53clb; Kumar Sriskandan 13cra; Travel Pictures 4b, 59cl; travelpix 78br; Terence Waeland 44bl; Westend61 GmbH/Werner Dieterich 49cl; World History Archive 8br.

Antwerp Zoo: Jonas Verhulst 56t.

Archiduc: Nathalie Du Four 79tl.

Archives du Musée Horta, Saint-Gilles, Bruxelles: Paul Louis 22ca,22crb, 22bl, 23tl, 23bc.

Bistro Christophe: 99cl.

Bridgeman Images: Patrick Lorette 41cla; Lukas - Art in Flanders VZW 30cla, 30crb, 30br.

Café d'Anvers: 107cra.

Comics Art Museum: 74t; Daniel Fouss 4cla, 26cl, 26-7, 27tl; © Hergé-Moulinsart /Daniel Fouss 27br.

Corbis: adoc-photos 40b; Atlantide Phototravel /Massimo Borchi 16tl; Christie's Images 42bc, 45tl; The Gallery Collection 44crb, 52t; Leemage 40c; Loop Images/Anna Stowe 105tl; Francis G. Mayer 44tl; Sutton Images/ Phipps 43tr; Sygma / Jacques Pavlovsky 42t.

© DACS 2016: Bl, ADAGP, Paris 19tl.

Design Museum Ghent: Phile Deprez 111cl.

Dreamstime.com: Alessandro0770 4cl; Amzphoto 16cr; Leonid Andronov 75bl; Bombaert 4clb; Gunold Brunbauer 50bl; Nicolas De Corte 60b; Sergey Dzyuba 4t, 55br; Emicristea 1, 35tc, 64b, 82tl, 88-9, 91crb, 102tl, 109br; Europhotos 2tl, 10-1, 73tr; Evgeniy Fesenko 17tr; Freesurf69 101tl; Roberto Atencia Gutierrez 94tl; Aija Lehtonen 67cl; Mikhail Markovskiy 9t; Mchudo 6bl; Martin Molcan 13tr; Monkey Business Images 62br; Neirfy 92bl; Olgacov 3tl, 70-1, 91tl; Parys 46t; Photogolfer 24-5, 109tl; Photowitch 92cra; Miroslav Pinkava 69cl; Ppy2010ha 61br; Dmitry Rukhlenko 28-7; Jozef Sedmak 34cl, 34bl, 34-5, 47tr; Olena Serditova 57cl; Siraanamwong 13bl; Suttipon 65tr; Tacna 73br; Tupungato 65cl; Wavybxl 77tr.

L'Ecailler du Palais Royal: 80cla.

Getty Images: ©Association des Architectes du CIC: Vanden Bossche sprl, CRV s.A., CDG sprl, Studiegroep D. Bontinck photo by Photonostop

RM/ Tibor Bognar 84br; LatinContent/Jorge Luis Alvarez Pupo 67br; Sylvain Sonne 3tr, 114-5.

Groot Vleeshuis: 112tr.

Historium Brugge: 97t.

Huis van Alijn: 110tl.

Huisbrouwerij De Halve Maan: 2tr, 38-9, 94tr.

Klarafestival: Sander Buyck 66t.

L'Ultime Atome: 87bl.

Maagdenhuismuseum : 104bc; Binnenkoer 64tr.

Musée d'Ixelles: 84cla.

Musée des Instruments de Musique: 12cl, 20cr, 21; Liesbeth Bonner 20br; Milo-Profi/Arthur Los 20clb.

Museum of Natural Sciences, Brussels: Th. Hubin 86tr.

Patrick Devos: 98bl.

Restaurant De Karmeliet: Heikki Verdurme 98tr.

Rex by Shutterstock: 4cra, 28clb, Colorsport 43clb.

Robert Harding Picture Library: Tibor Bognar 13br; Heinz Dieter Falkenstein 47cl, Marc De Ganck 57br; Jevgenija Pigozne 52bl; Gunter Kirsch 29tl; Martin Moxter 7tl; Peter Richardson 8tl; Phil Robinson 103cl, 105crb; Riccardo Sala 109c.

Royal Museum of Fine Arts of Belgium, Brussels: © DACS 2016 18-9; Johan Geleyns 18cl, 18b, 19cb, 73clb, 85cl.

Photo Scala, Florence: Bl, ADAGP, Paris /© DACS 2016 19tl.

Sips Cocktails: 107clb.

Stad Antwerpen: MAS/Filip Dujardin 49tr; Museum Ann de Stroom/Hugo Maertens 50crb; Museum Ann de Stroom 100tl; Museum Mayer van den Bergh 102br; Rubenshuis 36tr, 36cl, 36-7, 101crb, /Bart Huysmans 37crb, /Michel Wuyts 36br; Michel Wuyts 104tl.

STAM: 110br.

SuperStock: age fotostock/Sara Janini 9cr; Christie's Images Ltd 45br; DeAgostini 31br, 33c; Fine Art Images 31cl; Iberfoto 13c, 32, 33tl, 33cl, 33bl.

La Taverne du Passage: Dominique Rodenbach 81cr.

Van Buuren Museum: 83crb.

All other images © Dorling Kindersley
For further information see: www.dkimages.com

Cover

Front and spine: **Getty Images:** Jorg Greuel

Back: **Dreamstime.com:** Emicristea

Pull Out Map Cover

Getty Images: Jorg Greuel

All other images © Dorling Kindersley

For further information see:
www.dkimages.com

As a guide to abbreviations in visitor information blocks: **Adm** = *admission charge;* **DA** = *disabled access;* **D** = *dinner;* **L** = *lunch.*

Penguin
Random
House

Printed and bound in China

First published in Great Britain in 2004
by Dorling Kindersley Limited
345 Hudson Street, New York,
New York 10014

Copyright 2004, 2017 © Dorling
Kindersley Limited

A Penguin Random House Company

16 17 18 19 10 9 8 7 6 5 4 3 2 1

Reprinted with revisions 2006, 2008, 2010, 2012, 2014, 2017

A CIP catalogue record is available from the British Library.

ISSN 1479-344X
ISBN 9781 4654 5706 6

MIX
Paper from responsible sources
FSC™ C018179

SPECIAL EDITIONS OF DK TRAVEL GUIDES

DK Travel Guides can be purchased in bulk quantities at discounted prices for use in promotions or as premiums. We are also able to offer special editions and personalized jackets, corporate imprints, and excerpts from all of our books, tailored specifically to meet your own needs.

To find out more, please contact:

in the US
specialsales@dk.com

in the UK
travelguides@uk.dk.com

in Canada
specialmarkets@dk.com

in Australia
**penguincorporatesales@
penguinrandomhouse.com.au**

Phrase Book: French

In an Emergency

Help!	**Au secours!**	*oh sekoor*
Stop!	**Arrêtez!**	*aret-ay*
Call a doctor	**Appelez un medecin**	*apuh-lay uñ medsañ*
Call the police	**Appelez la police**	*apuh-lay lah pol-ees*
Call the fire brigade	**Appelez les pompiers**	*apuh-lay leh poñ-peeyay*
Where is the nearest telephone?	**Où est le téléphone le plus proche**	*oo ay luh tehlehfon luh ploo prosh*

Communication Essentials

Yes/No	**Oui/Non**	*wee/noñ*
Please	**S'il vous plaît**	*seel voo play*
Thank you	**Merci**	*mer-see*
Excuse me	**Excusez-moi**	*exkoo-zay mwah*
Hello	**Bonjour**	*boñzhoor*
Goodbye	**Au revoir**	*oh ruh-vwar*
Good evening	**Bon soir**	*boñ-swar*
morning	**Le matin**	*matañ*
afternoon	**L'apres-midi**	*l'apreh-meedee*
evening	**Le soir**	*swah*
yesterday	**Hier**	*eeyehr*
today	**Aujourd'hui**	*oh-zhoor-dwee*
tomorrow	**Demain**	*duhmañ*
here	**Ici**	*ee-see*
there	**Là bas**	*lah bah*
What?	**Quel/quelle?**	*kel, kel*
When?	**Quand?**	*koñ*
Why?	**Pourquoi?**	*poor-kwah*
Where?	**Où?**	*oo*

Useful Phrases

How do you do?	**Comment allez vous?**	*kom-moñ talay voo*
Very well, thank you	**Très bien, merci**	*treh byañ, mer-see*
How are you?	**Comment ça va?**	*kom-moñ sah vah*
See you soon	**À bientôt**	*ah byañ-toh*
That's fine	**Ça va bien**	*sah vah byañ*
Where is/are ...?	**Où est/sont ...?**	*ooh ay/soñ*
Which way to ...?	**Quelle est la direction pour ...?**	*kel ay lah deer-ek-syoñ poor*
Do you speak English?	**Parlez-vous anglais?**	*par-lay voo oñg-lay?*
I don't understand	**Je ne comprends pas**	*zhuh nuh kom-proñ pah*
I'm sorry	**Excusez-moi**	*exkoo-zay mwah*

Shopping

How much?	**C'est combien?**	*say kom-byañ*
I would like ...	**Je voudrais**	*zhuh voo-dray*
Do you have ...?	**Est-ce que vous avez ...?**	*es-kuh voo zavay*
Do you take credit cards?	**Est-ce que vous acceptez les cartes de crédit?**	*es-kuh voo zaksept-ay leh kart duh kreh-dee*
What time do you open/ close?	**À quelle heure vous êtes ouvert/ fermé?**	*ah kel urr voo zet oo-ver/ fermay*
this one	**celui-ci**	*suhl-wee see*
that one	**celui-là**	*suhl-wee lah*
expensive	**cher**	*shehr*
cheap	**pas cher, bon marché**	*pah shehr, boñ mar-shay*

size (clothing)	**la taille**	*tye*
white	**blanc**	*bloñ*
black	**noir**	*nwahr*
red	**rouge**	*roozh*
yellow	**jaune**	*zhownh*
green	**vert**	*vehr*
blue	**bleu**	*bluh*

Types of Shop

bakery	**la boulangerie**	*booloñ-zhuree*
bank	**la banque**	*boñk*
bookshop	**la librairie**	*lee-brehree*
butcher	**la boucherie**	*boo-shehree*
cake shop	**la pâtisserie**	*patee-sree*
chemist	**la pharmacie**	*farmah-see*
chip shop/stand	**la friterie**	*free-tuh-ree*
chocolate shop	**le chocolatier**	*shok-oh-lah-tyeh*
delicatessen	**la charcuterie**	*shah-koo-tuh-ree*
department store	**le grand magasin**	*groñ maga-zañ*
fishmonger	**la poissonerie**	*pwasson-ree*
greengrocer	**le marchand de légumes**	*mar-shoñ duh lay-goom*
hairdresser	**le coiffeur**	*kwafuhr*
market	**le marché**	*marsh ay*
newsagent	**le magasin de journaux/tabac**	*maga-zañ duh zhoor-no/ta-bak*
post office	**le bureau de poste**	*boo-roh duh pohst*
shop	**le magasin**	*maga-zañ*
supermarket	**le supermarché**	*soo-pehr-marshay*
travel agency	**l'agence de voyage**	*azhons duh vwayazh*

Sightseeing

art gallery	**la galérie d'art**	*galer-ree dart*
bus station	**la gare routière**	*gahr roo-tee-yehr*
cathedral	**la cathédrale**	*katay-dral*
church	**l'église**	*aygleez*
closed on public	**fermeture jour ferié**	*fehrmeh-tur zhoor fehree-ay*
garden	**le jardin**	*zhah-dañ*
library	**la bibliothèque**	*beebleeo-tek*
museum	**le musée**	*moo-zay*
railway station	**la gare (SNCB)**	*gahr (es-en-say-bay)*
tourist office	**les informations**	*uñ-for-mah-syoñ*
town hall	**l'hôtel de ville**	*ohtel duh vil*
train	**le train**	*trañ*

Staying in a Hotel

Do you have a vacant room?	**est-ce que vous avez une chambre?**	*es-kuh voo zavay oon shambr*
double room	**la chambre à deux personnes**	*shambr ah duh per-son*
with double bed	**avec un grand lit**	*ah-vek uñ groñ lee*
twin room	**la chambre à deux lits**	*shambr ah duhlee*
single room	**la chambre à une personne**	*shambr ah oon pehr-son*
room with a bath	**la chambre avec salle de bain**	*shambr ah-vek sal duh bañ*
shower	**une douche**	*doosh*
I have a reservation	**J'ai fait une reservation**	*zhay fay oon ray-zehrva-syoñ*

Eating Out

Have you got a table?	Avez vous une table libre?	avay-voo oon tahbl leebr
I would like to reserve a table	Je voudrais réserver une table	zhuh voo-dray rayzehr-vay oon tahbl
The bill, please	L'addition, s'il vous plait	l'adee-syoñ, seel voo play
I am a vegetarian	Je suis végétarien	zhuh swee vezhay-tehryañ
waiter/ waitress	Monsieur/ Mademoiselle	muh-syur/ mad-uh-mwah-zel
menu	le menu	men-oo
wine list	la carte des vins	lah kart-deh vañ
glass	verre	vehr
bottle	la bouteille	boo-tay
knife	le couteau	koo-toh
fork	la fourchette	for-shet
spoon	la cuillère	kwee-yehr
breakfast	le petit déjeuner	puh-tee day-zhuh-nay
lunch	le déjeuner	day zhuh-nay
dinner	le dîner	dee-nay
main course	le grand plat	groñ plah
starter	l'hors d'oeuvre	or duhvr
dessert	le dessert	deh-zehrt
dish of the day	le plat du jour	plah doo joor
bar	le bar	bah
café	le café	ka-fay
rare	saignant	say nyoñ
medium	à point	ah pwañ
well done	bien cuit	byañ kwee

Menu Decoder

agneau	ahyoh	lamb
ail	eye	garlic
asperges	ahs-pehrj	asparagus
bar/loup de mer	bah/loo duh mare	bass
bière	byahr	beer
boeuf	buhf	beef
brochet	brosh-ay	pike
café	kah-fay	coffee
café au lait	kah-fay oh lay	white coffee
caffe latte	kah-fay lat uh	milky coffee
canard	kanar	duck
cerf/chevreuil	surf/shev-roy	venison
chicon	shee-koñ	Belgian endive
chocolat chaud	shok-oh-lah shoh	hot chocolate
choux de Bruxelles	shoo duh broocksell	Brussels sprouts
coquille Saint-Jacques	kok-eel sañ jak	scallop
crêpe	crayp	pancake
crevette	kreh-vet	prawn
dorade	doh-rad	sea bream
eau	oh	water
epinard	eypeenar	spinach
faisant	feh-zoñ	pheasant
frites	freet	chips/fries
fruits	frwee	fruit
gauffre	gohfr	waffle
hareng	ah-roñ	herring
haricots	arrykoh	haricot beans
haricots verts	arrykoh vehr	green beans
homard	oh-ma	lobster
huitre	weetr	oyster
jus d'orange	zhoo doh-ronj	orange juice
légumes	lay-goom	vegetables
limonade	lee-moh-nad	lemonade
lotte	lot	monkfish
moule	mool	mussel
poisson	pwah-ssoñ	fish
pommes de terre	pom-duh tehr	potatoes
porc	por	pork
poulet	poo-lay	chicken
raie	ray	skate
saumon	soh-moñ	salmon
thé	tay	tea
thon	toñ	tuna
truffe	troof	truffle
truite	trweet	trout
veau	voh	veal
viande	vee-yand	meat
vin	vañ	wine
vin maison	vañ may-soñ	house wine

Numbers

0	zéro	zeh-roh
1	un, une	uñ, oon
2	deux	duh
3	trois	trwah
4	quatre	katr
5	cinq	sañk
6	six	sees
7	sept	set
8	huit	weet
9	neuf	nurf
10	dix	dees
11	onze	oñz
12	douze	dooz
13	treize	trehz
14	quatorze	katorz
15	quinze	kañz
16	seize	sehz
17	dix-sept	dees-set
18	dix-huit	dees-zweet
19	dix-neuf	dees-znurf
20	vingt	vañ
21	vingt-et-un	vañ ay uhn
30	trente	tront
40	quarante	karoñt
50	cinquante	sañkoñt
60	soixante	swahsoñt
70	septante	setoñt
80	quatre-vingt	katr-vañ
90	quatre-vingt-dix/ nonante	katr vañ dees/ nonañ
100	cent	soñ
1000	mille	meel
1,000,000	million	miyoñ

Time

What is the time?	Quelle heure est-il?	kel uhr eh-til
one minute	une minute	oon mee-noot
one hour	une heure	oon uhr
half an hour	une demi heure	oon duhf-mee uhr
half past one	une heure et demi	oon uhr ay duh-mee
a day	un jour	zhuhr
a week	une semaine	suh-man
a month	un mois	mwah
a year	une année	annay
Monday	lundi	luñ-dee
Tuesday	mardi	mahr-dee
Wednesday	mercredi	mehrkruh-dee
Thursday	jeudi	zhuh-dee
Friday	vendredi	voñdruh-dee
Saturday	samedi	sam-dee
Sunday	dimanche	dee-moñsh

Phrase Book: Dutch

In an Emergency

Help!	**Help!**	*help*
Stop!	**Stop!**	*stop*
Call a doctor!	**Haal een dokter!**	*haal uhndok-tur*
Call the police!	**Roep de politie!**	*roop duh poe-leet-see*
Call the fire brigade!	**Roep de brandweer!**	*roop duh brahnt-vheer*
Where is the nearest telephone?	**Waar ist de dichtsbijzijnde telefoon?**	*vhaar iss duh dikst-baiy-zaiyn duh tay-luh-foan*
Where is the nearest hospital?	**Waar ist het dichtsbijzijnde ziekenhuis**	*vhaar iss het dikst-baiy-zaiyn -duh zee-kuh-hows*

Communication Essentials

Yes	**Ja**	*yaa*
No	**Nee**	*nay*
Please	**Alstublieft**	*ahls-tew-bleeft*
Thank you	**Dank u**	*dhank-ew*
Excuse me	**Pardon**	*pahr-don*
Hello	**Hallo**	*haa-lo*
Goodbye	**Dag**	*dahgh*
Good night	**Goedenacht**	*ghoot-e-naakt*
morning	**Morgen**	*mor-ghugh*
afternoon	**Middag**	*mid-dahgh*
evening	**Avond**	*av-vohnd*
yesterday	**Gisteren**	*ghis-tern*
today	**Vandaag**	*van-daagh*
tomorrow	**Morgen**	*mor-ghugh*
here	**Hier**	*heer*
there	**Daar**	*daar*
What?	**Wat?**	*vhat*
When?	**Wanneer?**	*vhan-eer*
Why?	**Waarom?**	*vhaar-om*
Where?	**Waar?**	*vhaar*
How?	**Hoe?**	*hoo*

Useful Phrases

How are you?	**Hoe gaat het ermee?**	*hoo ghaat het er-may*
Very well, thank you	**Heel goed, dank u**	*hayl ghoot, dhank ew*
How do you do?	**Hoe maakt u het?**	*hoo maakt ew het*
See you soon	**Tot ziens**	*tot zeens*
That's fine	**Prima**	*pree-mah*
Where is/are …?	**Waar is/zijn …?**	*vhaar iss/zayn*
How far is it to …?	**Hoe ver is het naar …?**	*hoo vehr iss het nar*
How do I get to …?	**Hoe kom ik naar …?**	*hoo kom ik nar*
Do you speak English?	**Spreekt u engels?**	*spraykt uw eng-uhls*
I don't understand	**Ik snap het niet**	*ik snahp het neet*
Could you speak slowly?	**Kunt u langzamer praten?**	*kuhnt ew lahng-zarmer-praat-tuh*
I'm sorry	**Sorry**	*sorry*

Shopping

I'm just looking	**Ik kijk alleen even**	*ik kaiyk alleyn ay-vuh*
How much does this cost?	**Hoeveel kost dit?**	*hoo-vayl kost dit*
What time do you open?	**Hoe laat gaat u open?**	*hoo laat ghaat ew opuh*
What time do you close?	**Hoe laat gaat u dicht?**	*hoo laat ghaat ew dikht*
I would like …	**Ik wil graag …**	*ik vhil ghraakh*
Do you have …?	**Heeft u …?**	*hayft ew*
Do you take credit cards?	**Neemt u credit cards aan?**	*naymt ew credit cards aan?*
Do you take travellers' cheques?	**Neemt u reischeques aan?**	*naymt ew raiys-sheks aan*
This one	**Deze**	*day-zuh*
That one	**Die**	*dee*
expensive	**duur**	*dewr*
cheap	**goedkoop**	*ghoot-koap*
size	**maat**	*maat*
white	**wit**	*vhit*
black	**zwart**	*zvhahrt*
red	**rood**	*roat*
yellow	**geel**	*ghayl*
green	**groen**	*ghroon*
blue	**blauw**	*blah-ew*

Types of Shop

antiques shop	**antiekwinkel**	*ahn-teek-vhin-kul*
bakery	**bakkerij**	*bah-ker-aiy*
bank	**bank**	*bahnk*
bookshop	**boekwinkel**	*book-vhin-kul*
butcher	**slagerij**	*slaakh-er-aiy*
cake shop	**banketbakkerij**	*bahnk-et-bahk-er-aiy*
chip stop/stand	**patatzaak**	*pah-taht-zak*
chemist/ drugstore	**apotheek**	*ah-poe-taiyk*
delicatessen	**delicatessen**	*daylee-kah-tes-suh*
department store	**warenhuis**	*vhaah-uh-houws*
fishmonger	**viswinkel**	*viss-vhin-kul*
greengrocer	**groenteboer**	*ghroon-tuh-boor*
hairdresser	**kapper**	*kah-per*
market	**markt**	*mahrkt*
newsagent	**krantenwinkel**	*krahn-tuh-vhin-kul*
post office	**postkantoor**	*pohst-kahn-tor*
supermarket	**supermarkt**	*sew-per-mahrkt*
tobacconist	**sigarenwinkel**	*see-ghaa-ruh-vhin-kul*
travel agent	**reisburo**	*raiys-bew-roa*

Sightseeing

art gallery	**gallerie**	*ghaller-ée*
bus station	**busstation**	*buhs-stah-shown*
bus ticket	**kaartje**	*kaar-tyuh*
cathedral	**kathedraal**	*kah-tuh-draal*
church	**kerk**	*kehrk*
closed on public holidays	**op feestdagen gesloten**	*op fayst-daa-ghuh ghuh-slow-tuh*
day return	**dagretour**	*dahgh-ruh-tour*
garden	**tuin**	*touwn*
library	**bibliotheek**	*bee-bee-yo-tayk*
museum	**museum**	*mew-zay-um*
railway station	**station**	*stah-shown*
return ticket	**retourtje**	*ruh-tour-tyuh*
single journey	**enkeltje**	*eng-kuhl-tyuh*
tourist information	**dienst voor toerisme**	*deenst vor tor-ism*
town hall	**stadhuis**	*staht-houws*
train	**trein**	*traiyn*

Staying in a Hotel

double room with double bed	**een twees persoons-kamer met een twee persoonsbed**	*uhn tvhays per-soans- ka-mer met uhn tvhay per-soans beht*
single room	**eenpersoons-kamer**	*ayn-per-soans kaa-mer*

twin room	een kamer met een lits-jumeaux	uhn kaa-mer met uhn lee-zjoo-moh
room with a bath/shower	kaamer met bad/ douche	kaa-mer met baht/doosh
Do you have a vacant room?	Zijn er nog kamers vrij?	zaiyn er nokh kaa-mers vray
I have a reservation	Ik heb gereserveerd	ik hehp ghuh-ray-sehr-veert

Eating Out

Have you got a table?	Is er een tafel vrij?	iss ehr uhn tah-fuhl vraiy
I would like to reserve a table	Ik wil een tafel reserveren	ik vhil uhn tah-fel ray sehr-veer- uh
The bill, please	De rekening, alstublieft	duh ray-kuh-ning ahls-tew-bleeft
I am a vegetarian	Ik ben vegetariër	ik ben fay-ghuh-taahr-ee-er
waitress/waiter	serveerster/ ober	sehr-veer-ster/oh-ber
menu	de kaart	duh kaahrt
wine list	de wijnkaart	duh vhaiyn-kart
glass	het glass	het ghlahss
bottle	de fles	duh fless
knife	het mes	het mess
fork	de vork	duh fork
spoon	de lepel	duh lay-pul
breakfast	het ontbijt	het ont-buiyt
lunch	de lunch	duh lernsh
dinner	het diner	het dee-nay
main course	het hoofdgerecht	het hoaft-ghuh-rekht
starter, first course	het voorgerecht	het vhor-ghuh-rekht
dessert	het nagerecht	het naa-ghuh-rekht
dish of the day	het dagschotel	het dahg-skhoa-tel
bar	het cafe	het kaa-fay
café	het eetcafe	het ayt-kaa-fay
rare	rare	"rare"
medium	medium	"medium"
well done	doorbakken	door-bah-kuh

Menu Decoder

aardappels	aard-uppuhls	potatoes
asperges	as-puhj	asparagus
bier	beeh	beer
chocola	sho-koh-laa	chocolate
eend	aynt	duck
fazant	fay-zanh	pheasant
forel	foh-ruhl	trout
frietjes	free-tyuhs	chips/fries
fruit/vruchten	vroot/vrooh-tuh	fruit
garnaal	gar-nall	prawn
groenten	ghroon-tuh	vegetables
haring	haa-ring	herring
hertenvlees	hair-ten-flayss	venison
kalfsvlees	karfs-flayss	veal
kip	kip	chicken
knoflook	knoff-loak	garlic
koffie	coffee	coffee
kreeft	krayft	lobster
lamsvlees	lahms-flayss	lamb
lotte/zeeduivel	lot/scafuhdul	monkfish
mineraalwater	meener-aahl-vhaater	mineral water
mossel	moss-uhl	mussel
oester	ouhs-tuh	oyster
pannekoek	pah-nuh-kook	pancake
princesbonen	prins ess buh-nun	green beans

rog	rog	skate
rundvlees	ruhnt-flayss	beef
Sint Jacoboester/ Jacobsschelp	sind-yakob-ouhs-tuh/ yakob-scuhlp	scallop
snijbonen	snee-buh-nun	string beans
snoek	snoek	pike
spinazie	spin-a-jee	spinach
spruitjes	spruhr-tyuhs	Brussels sprouts
thee	tay	tea
tonijn	tuhn-een	tuna
truffel	truh-fuhl	truffle
varkensvlees	vahr-kuhns-flayss	pork
verse jus	vehr-suh zjhew	fresh orange juice
vis	fiss	fish
vlees	flayss	meat
wafel	vaff-uhl	waffle
water	vhaa-ter	water
wijn	vhaiyn	wine
witloof	vit-lurf	Belgian endive/chicory
zalm	sahlm	salmon
zeebars	see-buhr	seabass
zeebrasem	zee-brah-sum	sea bream

Numbers

1	een	ayn
2	twee	tvhay
3	drie	dree
4	vier	feer
5	vijf	faiyf
6	zes	zess
7	zeven	zay-vuh
8	acht	ahklit
9	negen	nay-guh
10	tien	teen
11	elf	elf
12	twaalf	tvhaalf
13	dertien	dehr-teen
14	veertien	feer-teen
15	vijftien	faiyf-teen
16	zestien	zess-teen
17	zeventien	zayvuh-teen
18	achtien	ahkh-teen
19	negentien	nay ghuh-tien
20	twintig	tvhin-tukh
21	eenentwintig	aynuh-tvhin-tukh
30	dertig	dehr-tukh
40	veertig	feer-tukh
50	vijftig	faiyf-tukh
60	zestig	zess-tukh
70	zeventig	zay-vuh-tukh
80	tachtig	tahkh-tukh
90	negentig	nayguh-tukh
100	honderd	hohn-durt
1000	duizend	douw-zuhnt
1,000,000	miljoen	mill-yoon

Time

one minute	een minuut	uhn meen-ewt
one hour	een uur	uhn ewr
half an hour	een half uur	een hahlf uhr
half past one	half twee	hahlf twee
a day	een dag	uhn dahgh
a week	een week	uhn vhayk
a month	een maand	uhn maant
a year	een jaar	uhn jaar
Monday	maandag	maan-dahgh
Tuesday	dinsdag	dins-dahgh
Wednesday	woensdag	vhoons-dahgh
Thursday	donderdag	donder-dahgh
Friday	vrijdag	vraiy-dahgh
Saturday	zaterdag	zaater-duhgh
Sunday	zondag	zon-dahgh

Brussels Selected Street Index